N
H
CA

A Practical guide

PAT COLEBY

NATURAL HORSE CARE

A Practical Guide

hachette
AUSTRALIA

Published in Australia and New Zealand in 2008
by Hachette Australia
(an imprint of Hachette Australia Pty Limited)
Level 17, 207 Kent Street, Sydney NSW 2000
www.hachette.com.au

Reprinted 2009, 2010

First published in 1989 by Kangaroo Press Pty Ltd
Revised editions published in 1992, 1994, 1995, 1997, 1998, 1999
by Grassroots Publishing Pty Ltd
Eighth edition published in 2003
by Thomas C. Lothian Pty Ltd.

Copyright © Pat Coleby 1989, 2003, 2008

This book is copyright. Apart from any fair dealing for the use
of private study, research, criticism or review permitted under
the Copyright Act 1968, no part may be stored or reproduced
by any process without prior written permission. Enquiries should
be made to the publisher.

National Library of Australia
Cataloguing-in-Publication data:

Coleby, Pat.
Natural Horse Care

ISBN 978 0 7336 2294 6

1. Horses – Nutrition – Requirements.
2. Horses – Feeding and feeds.
3. Horses – Health. I. Title.

636.1085

Cover design by Luke Causby
Cover photograph courtesy of Getty Images
Text design by John Van Loon
Digital production by Bookhouse, Sydney
Illustrations by Debbie Emeny and Anita Mertzlin
Printed in Australia by Griffin Press, Adelaide, an Accredited ISO AS/NZS 14001:2004
Environmental Management System printer

FSC
Mixed Sources
Product group from well-managed
forests and other controlled sources

Cert no. SGS-COC-005088
www.fsc.org
© 1996 Forest Stewardship Council

The paper this book is printed on is certified by the © 1996
Forest Stewardship Council A.C. (FSC). Griffin Press holds
FSC chain of custody SGS-COC-005088. FSC promotes
environmentally responsible, socially beneficial and
economically viable management of the world's forests.

Contents

Preface

This book is not, and was never intended to be, a manual of horse management. But as each updated edition comes out, I find myself having to cover that field more and more. There are many excellent books on the care of feet and teeth, and the methods of getting horses fit. But this book aims to show how horses can be kept in the best health possible by making sure they get the right feed. Chapter ten, which deals with conditioning, was added for the second edition due to repeated enquiries.

Many people with one or two horses have grown up in an era when there was little information on the subject. I spent hours in my youth doing miles of slow work with racehorses, hunters and showjumpers. A section on recuperation after damage or injury is included in this edition as an extension to chapter ten.

My association with horses goes back well over seventy years to before the days of chemical farming and the approach to prescribing drugs so largely used today. Many of the troubles we have now were unheard of in those days. In racing stables, the staple diet was enough to keep horses in optimum health, and the trainer I worked for in the United Kingdom topped the trainers list again and again.

Basically, I would class myself as a frustrated vet. At fifteen years of age, after obtaining the necessary educational standard, I announced to my family that I was going to be a vet (after much preliminary study had been done on the quiet). It was firmly vetoed. Children obeyed their parents in those days — but from that day on, I did not miss any opportunities for doctoring an animal or helping the local vets.

Working in a top racing yard from the bottom up did nothing to quench my enthusiasm, in spite of getting 'dropped' by the horses — usually rather hard — with monotonous regularity at first. I had ridden all my life and hunted over some of the toughest country in the United Kingdom, but racehorses were a whole new ball game! I was also lucky that the age of drugs and blood tests had not yet arrived. We had to observe our animals and note any changes in feeding or other habits and learn from it. My boss was possibly the greatest horsemaster of his era, and if you were so inclined, there was much to be learned.

Emigration to Australia in 1959 with an ailing husband and an expanding family did not prevent me from helping the landlords with their sheep, cattle and horses. The University of Melbourne were the district vets, and Dr V Sloss, teaching vet there for many years, taught me a great deal. He allowed me access to veterinary medication for the locals, as long as I administered it. He knew full well few people in the bush would call a vet in those days. Various disasters occurred with the conventional drugs that the University used on goats. Sheep were the only yardstick they had and no one really knew goats' requirements then. This made me look for other answers.

It would take too long here to describe how I realised minerals and vitamins were the key to many of the problems, but, when I did, it seemed almost too simple. The immense satisfaction in saving cases that had been given up — curing so-called incurable cases of mastitis, or a pony (destined to be shot) with a badly cracked shoulder belonging to the landlord — was all the encouragement I needed.

Fairly soon the district realised that I was cheaper than a vet (being free!) and I would be called out at the most unseasonable hours to pull lambs out of sheep, rescue foundered horses, and treat snakebitten and injured stock of all kinds.

When I published my first book (on goats) and began writing magazine articles and giving lectures at various organic and farming seminars, I would often find myself on the end of a telephone explaining to the caller what could be wrong with their horse, cow, goat, dog or cat, or occasionally even rabbit! The calls now come from all over Australia, New Zealand, the United States and the United Kingdom. I spend many more hours answering voluminous letters detailing symptoms that frankly have me horrified. They routinely say, 'My vet says there is nothing that can be done' and frankly, having heard the symptoms, too often I agree heartily. However nature is pretty remarkable — give it half a chance sometimes and it surprises everybody. We do not lose too many.

Several horses given up by the racing industry are now happily back in training again. Three wretched thoroughbreds in a horrible mess mentally and physically, were bought by my son at killing prices then restored to the workforce so much improved in condition and outlook that they were unrecognisable to their previous owners.

Since the first edition of this book in 1989, at least nineteen or more ailments have been added to the list. In Australia I find the need for supplementary minerals grows more not less.

Even more importantly, the land has to be rescued from continuing degradation, and the soil remineralised, or some of the horses cannot be saved. It is now not enough just to feed the minerals in the fodder and ignore the land — this does not work. The grass and hay that is grown *must* be top quality mineralwise too.

I hope that this book will show trainers, breeders and horsekeepers of all kinds the consequences when horses fail to obtain the required minerals and vitamins, and the almost unbelievable improvement when they do, often rectifying problems that were considered hopeless. I have been fortunate to know many vets and horsemasters of great wisdom, and owe them an incalculable debt of gratitude for sharing their knowledge so freely.

Here is a short anecdote in conclusion. A stud belonging to a friend has been using the methods I suggest for three years. When her first horse to be bred under that regime went into training, the horse dentist came to do its teeth. He wanted to know why the filly had teeth that were as hard as those of a four-year-old. He had met his first young horse with properly developed teeth and therefore bones to match!

In 2001, the first American edition of *Natural Horse Care* came out. Since the first edition of this book in 1989, I have had countless enquiries from the United States, Europe and New Zealand about complaints similar to those suffered by horses in Australia — land degradation now seems to be almost universal.

Pat Coleby
Maldon, Victoria

1 Soil deficiencies

Causes and results

Australia appears to be the only country in the world —
with the exception of one or two localities such as the Texas
Panhandle, Wales and Scandanavia — where there are serious inherent soil deficiencies. The minerals most usually lost
from a millennium of leaching, or as has happened in Wales,
from haphazard surface mining, are calcium and magnesium.
Iodine is another victim of leaching and in most cases iodine
and magnesium, in particular, are in very short supply all over
Australia.

Nowadays, in any country where modern chemical farming is still practised, there will be induced deficiencies of
iodine as well as many major and trace minerals. This is
due generally to the acidifying and/or inhibiting action
of artificial manures and fertilisers. In the horse world these

deficiencies are particularly serious. It does not seem to matter whether it is Australia, the United States, United Kingdom or Europe.

A soil scientist named Schuphan conducted tests over a period of fifteen years at the Haughley Experimental Centre in the United Kingdom at the end of World War Two. He established that twenty-eight per cent of minerals and vitamins were missing from the finished product when chemical farming methods were used. In organic (mixed) farming all these essentials were available to the user of the crop, whether it was grass, cereal or roots. Recently, there have been sporadic attempts to duplicate these figures and the results only vary in a few decimal points from Schuphan's early efforts.

In Australia, soil analyses from widely differing areas all show deficiencies in calcium and/or magnesium and sulphur to a greater or lesser extent. On the other hand, the average soil analysis in other countries shows adequate levels in most of these minerals. This probably explains the excellence of many of the racehorses that are reared overseas. Lack of calcium and/or magnesium is the major cause of leg and bone troubles, as will be seen in chapter eight. Shin soreness, for example, was not a problem in the racing industry in the United Kingdom in the mid-1900s. In fact, it was unheard of.

Nature usually provides an answer; in this case, it is lime deposits in the form of gypsum, lime or dolomite, made up of calcium sulphate, calcium carbonate, or calcium and magnesium, respectively. There are a number of dolomite mines in Australia producing good grade material. Dolomite is made up of calcium and magnesium, usually in the ratio of two thirds calcium to one third magnesium. In Australia, we also have a more expensive product called magnesite (keiserite in the United Kingdom), which has equal amounts of the two minerals.

At no time should any lime mineral be spread on paddocks

until an analysis shows the actual levels of calcium/magnesium and/or gypsum. Those minerals *must* be kept in balance and the analysis must include the full readout as shown in the SWEP example in the next chapter. Nor, in grazing paddocks, should the amount spread in one year exceed two tonnes to the hectare. Gypsum and dolomite can be included to bring the amount up to about 2.5 tonnes. It should be no more than that, no matter how low the lime mineral levels, and for grazing, the minerals *must* be brought up gradually. Consult chapter two — the CEC (Cation Exchange) governs how much may be spread in one year.

Other minerals, usually known as trace minerals, may also be deficient either inherently or because chemical farming methods have been practised. These include boron, copper, cobalt, zinc and selenium. Iodine, already mentioned, is not strictly a mineral and cannot therefore be shown on a mineral readout. It is often missing — it can also be inhibited by heavy feeding of legumes, as will be shown later in this book — and its presence is one hundred per cent important (see chapter four).

Sulphur is another casualty of modern farming. Normally this mineral would be adequately supplied in a horse's diet by bran or rolled wheat, of which it should be a natural component. Again our technology has over-run itself, and the use of triple superphosphate and subclover to revitalise the soil in the wheat-growing areas has, according to the CSIRO, made sulphur totally unavailable. Sulphur-deficient horses are inclined to suffer from exterior parasites and, according to the CSIRO *Rural Research Bulletin* and, more seriously, Dr Richard A Passwaters in the United States, without sulphur they cannot assimilate selenium. The amino acids of sulphur — cysteine and methionine particularly — are necessary for this synthesis.

For these reasons, much of the feed we buy for our horses

is deficient in many, if not all of the necessary nutrients, and some of it is actively harmful. For example, feed too high in iron means that all the vitamin E in the horse's system may be destroyed. Feed too high in salt means that potassium may suffer a similar fate depending on iron levels, otherwise the high salt may cause oedema. Both vitamin E and potassium are absolutely essential for sound, healthy horses, particularly if they are to be used for sustained activity like racing, eventing or dressage without succumbing to problems. A study of the soil analysis, a fairly usual sample, in chapter two, will show that iron and sodium are often above the desired level or badly out of balance.

Another effect of an imbalance in soil nutrients is that an excess of one will lock up others, making them unavailable to the user. For example, excessively high phosphorus will lock up calcium and magnesium, and the effects of too much iron and salt have already been explained. Therefore, if the fodder is grown on soil that is badly out of balance minerally, it can lead to ill health in the animal that eats it.

There are many books on this subject for those who wish to learn further, but much of the information is only just beginning to be fully understood. For example, nearly all so-called infectious diseases appear to be quite easily controlled by balancing the minerals in a horse's diet. When milking animals like cows and goats, mastitis may be avoided by ensuring that the beasts receive supplementary dolomite (dolomitic lime) in their bail rations. Footrot in cloven-hoofed animals, and abscesses and seedy toe in horses, can be virtually eliminated if they are all receiving their full copper requirements. When the animal is correctly supplemented these infections just do not occur, even when there are predisposing factors. Sheep farmers who are feeding organic minerals in as natural a form as possible report an amazing improvement in overall health, wool quality and an almost complete absence of many so-called disease conditions that had previously plagued them, particularly worm problems. Horse owners have been heard to complain that life is almost dull without the recurrent disease conditions cropping up.

Unfortunately, soil deficiencies appear to be increasing. Selenium deficiencies were fairly rare in the 1970s and '80s, but now many new areas lacking in the mineral are being discovered and the unavailability of sulphur is the main cause of the problem.

When my family came to Australia in the late 1950s, the thoroughbred stock horses we used for stock work went very well on pasture. Then, minerals did not seem to be a problem, but by 1965 we were running dolomite through the feed a couple of times a week and by the seventies we were giving the horses a daily dose with sulphur and copper. In the early 1970s, a thoroughbred mare of ours went down with colitis X (see chapter eight). Fast action by a Welsh vet working at the University of Melbourne saved her life (and her foal in utero). He said it was caused by a complete absence of minerals in her system. From then on, we fed them all — always.

2 Analysing soil

There is a totally independent firm in Australia at present that produces an easily understood soil analysis, which not only gives the amounts present but those that *should* be there. Horse owners should understand that the desirable levels are governed by the CEC (the Cation Exchange Capacity). Many people (including me initially) have difficulty with this; they enquire why the desired level on their land differs from the example shown in this or any other of my books. In simple terms, the ability of the soil to hold on and then release cations from the clay particles is called the soil's Cation Exchange Capacity, or its CEC. I have seen the CEC as high as sixty and as low as two or less. Horses are expected to live on both areas!

The analysing firm is listed in the Appendix. The average

cost of a soil analysis is (with GST) $110, with a further $11 for total (locked up) phosphorus (P), the same for total aluminium and so on. I expect my clients to do the total phosphorus analysis, as it is very important when sorting out health problems. Thus the full cost comes to $121. This of course is subject to change (usually just after a book is published!).

The subsequent printout that will arrive about eight or nine days after sending up the sample, will show clearly those minerals that are in short supply, out of balance and, more importantly, the desired level required (according to the CEC). These days there are agents for mineral fertilisers within reach of most localities, and they can arrange top-dressing when it is needed — which it has been in all the cases that I have seen.

It is also possible to have a foliage (tissue) analysis done on the pasture. The company listed in the Appendix can also do this. The only drawback to this method is that the tissue analysis can vary quite considerably according to the time of year, and in certain conditions can lie. According to the American agronomist Neal Kinsey, plants can, and do, show a magnesium deficiency where one does not exist in the soil, for example. This can mean a deficiency or an excess; plants cannot always differentiate. So for this reason a soil audit *must* come first. In pasture farming, I advise having only the soil done initially (with the total phosphorus), so that one can start the work of paddock regeneration.

Soil analysis seems preferable because the level of the minerals remains fairly constant in the soil, although there can be slight variations in the pH (acid/alkali balance) according to the time of year and rainfall. On the next page is a copy of an analysis from a pretty average farm in Australia; this farm bred and worked horses; we had ongoing problems until the soil was fully balanced, and stringhalt was the worst problem originally (see chapter eight).

Report on sample of soil

Items		Result	Desirable level
Colour: dark grey			
Texture: fine sandy clay loam, light			
pH (1:5 water)		5.1	
pH (1:5 01M CL2)		4.5	
Electrical conductivity	EC us/cm	79	<300
Total soluble salt	TSS ppm	260.7	< 900
Available calcium	Ca ppm	242	1303
Available magnesium	Mg ppm	54	138
Available sodium	Na ppm	32.2	<110
Available hydrogen	H ppm	74	19
Available nitrogen	N ppm	10	20
Available phosphorus	P ppm	21.0	20
Available potassium	K ppm	148.2	110
Available sulphur	S ppm	9.3	3–5
Available copper	Cu ppm	1.20	2
Available zinc	Zn ppm	5.80	3–5
Available iron	Fe ppm	365	>20
Available manganese	Mn ppm	25	>20
Available cobalt	Ca ppm	0.60	>0.5–0.7
Available molybdenum	Mo ppm	0.30	0.5–0.7
Available boron	B ppm	0.20	0.4–0.6
Total organic matter	OM%	4.8	3–4
Total phosphorus	TP ppm	244	
Extractable aluminium	AL ppm	NR	
Total nitrogen	N%	NR	
Cation exchange capacity	CEC	8.71	
Exch sodium percentage	ESP02.1	<5	
Calcium/magnesium ratio	Ca/Mg	2.69	2–4

Recommendations:

Gypsum	0 kg to the hectare
Lime	210 kg to the hectare
Dolomite	500 kg to the hectare

Trace minerals will not be relevant in this case, as the calcium pH is well below 5.8. At that level of acidity they would be lost if spread. Once the lime minerals are in balance, often many of the trace minerals come up near the desired level as well.

Copper	0.5 kg to the hectare
Zinc	0 kg to the hectare
Cobalt	0 kg to the hectare
Molybdenum	0.03 kg to the hectare
Iron	0.1 kg to the hectare
Manganese	0 kg to the hectare
Boron	0.2 kg to the hectare

These can be, where necessary, added to the feed.

The desired levels, as shown above, give the best amount for mixed pastures under reasonable rainfall conditions. These can vary. It takes many years to degrade the soil — the restoration can be achieved much faster. The unexpected bonus of this kind of reclamation project is not only the visible improvement of the pasture. Even before that becomes obvious, the improvement in the condition of horses grazing it will be apparent. In illnesses like stringhalt, for example, the cure does not work if the pasture has not been remineralised and the calcium (Ca) to magnesium (Mg) ratio balanced. In addition to this, it is important to know the trace mineral levels, as insufficient copper (Cu) can also have an effect on that particular condition.

On soils very low in calcium, it is totally inadvisable to apply more than two tonnes of lime to the hectare. Half a tonne of gypsum or dolomite can be added if required, but no more should be used (refer back to the section on CEC). Further application will have to be done in successive years. Large amounts of lime lock up the immediate magnesium (no matter how high it is in the soil) to the point where the animals become very ill.

In late 1997, I had to try and resuscitate a horse and a number of goats where this had been done. In each case, the advisor knew nothing of the reaction that takes place in animals grazing such a paddock. The tests had been processed in the United States and the recommendations used were quite valid for a crop paddock in that country. We were lucky not to lose the animals concerned. Another snag to having analyses done in the United States is that because of their often high magnesium, they do not understand how to work with very low levels.

After remineralisation, an aerator of some type may be used when the ground is wet enough (after 80 ml of rain). But this may turn out to be unnecessary, as soil compaction is caused almost entirely by lime levels that are out of balance.

Sour, depleted, degraded, overworked ground generally shows calcium and magnesium levels that are out of balance. The worst kinds of weeds and poorer quality grasses will be replaced by more nutritional species of both as the soil balance improves. Legumes and beneficial weeds like real dandelions will eventually appear and the health of the stock will improve accordingly. Even fireweed ceases to be a problem once remineralisation is started.

There are situations where an aerator *does* help, but I never believe in unnecessary work or expense. I own an aerator and it owes me nothing. I have used it off and on for about thirty years (when it is not out with one of my children). But frequently, once the soil is balanced, the necessity for an aerator is not so crucial. To use it on land that is already friable is a waste of time and might do actual damage. I try to persuade people to contract to have the job done, otherwise one is apt to have an expensive piece of machinery sitting idle.

When the pH is as low as the analysis in my example, do not even consider spreading trace elements, because they will be sulphated out and lost in the first rainstorm. When the pH improves after the lime minerals are balanced, calcium, magnesium and gypsum (calcium sulphate) come back into the food chain. I have seen this happen on a couple of the farms we have improved. On one, the cobalt, a very danger-ous mineral to have in low supply, was back in the food chain in eighteen months. On another, the copper went from 0.2 ppm to 8 ppm in about four to five years. At this level, all the stock on that paddock were in excellent health; interest-ingly enough though, they still looked for copper in their diets.

The hydrogen on the analysis is a very useful tool for me, as I rarely see any of the farms that belong to my far-flung clients. When soil reaches a certain stage of degeneration, the hydrogen ions take over and displace the necessary ones such as calcium, magnesium, potassium and phosphorus. This means abundance of the wrong types of weeds, some of which (capeweed and Smooth cat's ear) can cause conditions like stringhalt in very little time.

3 Improving and maintaining pastures

It is possible to assess the health of a pasture even before it is analysed. A preponderance of bracken, fireweed, dock, capeweed, buttercup, onion grass, oxalis, hoary cress, heliotrope — any or all of these — means that the soil is starved of humus (organic matter), and the calcium to magnesium ratio and/or the sulphur and pH are way out. The horse owner should realise that when the lime minerals are imbalanced, the paddock needs analysing so that the calcium, magnesium and/or gypsum can be replaced, otherwise it will not become healthy. A soil analysis (explained in chapter two) will show what reclamation measures will be needed.

Bracken is always the sign of poor, compacted soil low in potassium and lacking in soil nutrients. It is not necessary to spray to get rid of it; organic matter such as manure and compost, plus remineralisation and aerating get rid of it almost entirely in a year. In Europe, a little bracken in the paddock is considered to be medicinal and animals that need it are allowed to help themselves as they choose. However, turning an animal out into a paddock that is all bracken is *not* a good idea. I have seen it done with awful results. The cumulative poison in the bracken will cause damage and can wreck the liver.

It would be a waste of time and money at this stage to buy expensive seed and sow the paddock down. The seed might grow in the first year, but there would be no regeneration if conditions were unsuitable. Good quality grasses only grow in healthy, well-balanced soil, a fact that is rarely if ever pointed out by the people who sell the seed. A rough rule of thumb is that the hairy type of grasses are low in nutrients and of poor quality, while the harder, smoother grasses are of higher feed value. African-type grasses, with the exception of Flinders and Rhodes varieties, are *not* suitable, and cause big head and other similar conditions covered later in this book.

The first step is to have an analysis done and then top-dress with the required lime minerals to bring the calcium and magnesium into their correct ratio. The pH will follow. When the paddock is right, the pH should be around 6.5–7.0. People have said to me that all they need is a pH meter — wrong. At the ideal pH range it is still possible for the calcium and magnesium to be dangerously out of balance.

The use of a soil aerator will accelerate the improvement. On heavy soils, the Wallace/Yeomans type with feet that aerate about 18 cm below the surface is excellent. On light sandy soils, the roller kind with tynes sticking out is safer and will not cause erosion. I have found that after using a Wallace/Yeomans-type soil conditioner on really sour soil (after remineralisation), a recovery in the type of growth started within six months. Its action in renovating the soil appears to be equal to half a tonne of lime minerals (whichever are needed) per annum per hectare.

Another important thing to do is to replace the organic matter in the soil. Even quite healthy-looking paddocks can be lacking in humus (decayed vegetable matter in the ground) and will respond amazingly to being treated with natural, organic manures. This is what they receive from the horses and stock grazing on them.

Bracken only grows on depleted soils and ceases to be a problem as soon as the paddock is top-dressed with organic manure. I found this out by accident on one of our early farms that was one-thirds covered in bracken. As usual, I spread the manure from the sheds over the farm, wondering if there would be three-metre high bracken the next year. To my amazement, there was only a little weak growth from then on and the bracken ceased to be a problem. The farm had been fertilised with superphospate and muriate of potash every year for a long time, resulting in masses of poor quality grasses, weeds, blackberries and bracken.

It is best to compost manure first, but in starved Australian soils uncomposted horse, sheep or cow manure is better than nothing. Make sure that the manure has not come from stock which has had poisonous drenches.

Care should be taken in one's choice of manure. Chicken or pig manure from intensive systems using sawdust tends to acidify the soil. Rice hulls are better, but both types of manure should be thoroughly composted first. This also avoids contaminating the soil with the growth hormones and antibiotics sometimes used in chicken or pig farming. A very good commercial grower I was apprenticed to during and after World War Two would not allow chicken or pig manure to be used unless it had been composted for at least a year, preferably two. Sawdust-based manure can be used if the pH is monitored regularly and dolomite or lime spread at intervals following an analysis to counter any acidity.

Stable manure, slurry from cow or pig operations, and goat manure are all very good for pasture improvement. Uncomposted, it should only go out under a crop or on a paddock which is not being grazed prior to being shut up for hay. It must be remembered that no animal will touch herbage that has been treated with fresh manure until at least three months after it has been spread (unless it is starving).

After many years of spreading both horse and goat manure on paddocks, I have never found that an upsurge in the internal worm populations of either animal resulted. Possibly the reason is that the soil health is so improved by the practice that the earthworms, dung beetles and soil bacteria become very active in breaking down the manure. They then utilise it below the surface where it belongs, and stop faecal contamination. The difference in the pasture before and after applications of natural manure can be marked. The spring grass will become much thicker and be a deep green instead of the rather livid bright colour to which most of us have become accustomed in conventionally fertilised paddocks.

The soil aerator/conditioner can double as a sod-seeder when the soil has been improved enough to sow good grasses. However, this may not be necessary. One of the rewarding aspects of regenerating one's pasture is that species of grass that were not present at first suddenly reappear as the health of the soil suits them. This may sound unlikely, but it has happened on a number of farms under this program. The undesirables disappear and the good species take over.

In the United States, studies have found that unwanted couch grasses cease to be a problem once the pH reached a level of 6.0 and above.

In Australia, farmers with pastures badly contaminated by fireweed have found that a year after top-dressing the required lime minerals, the fireweed virtually disappears. If paddocks are so poor that horses are forced to eat fireweed, death will follow within eighteen months because it contains an alkaloid that destroys the liver. In a postmortem, the horse's liver presents a flat, dead appearance and the edges are scalloped.

There is an erroneous and widespread belief that the more clover there is in the pasture, the better it is. On the contrary, it can often be quite lethal. Excessive use of artificial fertilisers is usually the cause. Horses (or any other animal) grazing such a pasture rapidly become sick, and a host of illnesses related to calcium, magnesium and iodine deficiencies take over. Clover in a paddock should consist of no more than half the herbage present (as a maximum). Horses do not show any preference for clover and are only induced to eat too much if they are very hungry. Legumes are needed for nitrogen fixation, but a paddock too high in nitrogen is not healthy. Artificial nitrogen should not ever be used on paddocks where horses or other animals graze under any circumstances, if the stock are to remain healthy.

Another often-neglected aspect of pasture management is the provision of adequate stands of trees. These are obviously necessary for shade, but they also improve the health of the soil by bringing up nutrients from deep down. Trees also help to equalise the temperature, so that excesses of cold or heat are avoided. Fodder trees such as lucerne (tagasaste) and casuarinas can be planted with advantage. The former prefer well-drained or dry soils and will not grow with wet feet. They are also totally allergic to any form of glyphosate and can be used as an indicator of its presence. In wetter areas, willows make excellent fodder reserves and will grow quite happily with their roots in water.

In more fertile countries, horses, with the exception of brumbies and mustangs, rarely eat trees and leaves. But in Australia conditions can be very hard, and riding horses of all kinds will, if they get the chance, eat quite a few of the palatable trees and bushes. Make sure horses receive the copper they need, otherwise they will ringbark and kill the trees (copper appears to accumulate in bark). Horses, like sheep and cattle, will also eat very young trees and for that reason these must be safely fenced off at first.

4 Minerals

The saying, 'If a little is good, more must be better', does *not* apply to minerals, whether it is on the soil or in the body of a horse.

Use as basic a form of minerals as possible. It appears that the simpler the form of minerals in the diet, the better they are assimilated. I saw a herd of cattle in the United Kingdom that were being fed a large amount of mostly chelated, high-tech minerals of every kind. The cows were in a state of considerable ill health mainly due to liver malfunction. Their bilirubin (liver function test used in all living organisms) counts were below point five and they should have been seven. I suggested that the farmer make the change to a basic mixture we use here of dolomite, sulphur, copper and seaweed powder. The improvement, which began after four days, has

continued in all ages of beasts. The price comparison of the two regimes cheered the farmer up no end!

I have discussed this with many veterinary and medical professionals, and all came to the same conclusion, that chelated minerals are not safe to be ingested by mouth. (They were originally invented to be added to the blood.)

Proprietary licks and bullets

Various authorities have pointed out the uselessness of proprietary salt licks and blocks, as they never contain enough of the minerals that are really needed. On-farm supplementation, according to soil analyses, is suggested as the most economical method for correcting problems. The mixture I suggest below has proved successful for all species. Occasional additions are required, depending on the deficiencies noted in the analysis — cobalt and boron are the two most usual additions; usually about 25 g of each, if needed.

Bone-building minerals and vitamins

Horses must have sound bones. It should be remembered that four minerals and two vitamins are the *bare* essentials for healthy bones, and I am sure when we know more, there will be others as well. The minerals are:

Calcium and magnesium found naturally in dolomite;
Copper, in copper sulphate (twenty-seven per cent) or similar;
Boron — found naturally in seaweed meal, but if extra is needed it can be given as sodium borate (borax); and
Vitamins A and D, both found naturally in cod-liver oil.

Boron (B), in borax (sodium borate)

This is an essential trace mineral needed in very small amounts; it will damage the liver in excess. Calcium and magnesium will not be correctly utilised if it is missing, leading to arthritic-type problems.

In areas that are mapped as boron deficient, such as the country round Bendigo in Victoria, arthritis in all stock and most people is widespread. This is usually controlled by feeding either seaweed products which contain natural boron, or if this is not enough add 1 g a head per week of borax for goats and 3 g per head per week for the horses. Until this was done for my milking herd of goats and my horses, their creaking joints were audible as they walked around the paddocks.

This deficiency would have eventually shown up as arthritis or some other bone or joint problem.

Unfortunately, soils under conventional management seem to be losing this mineral at an ever-increasing rate in Australia. I have quite a few of my clients' horses on maintenance doses of boron, at 3–4 g per week.

Calcium (Ca)

This is found as calcium carbonate in ground limestone, but the safest way to use it is from dolomite. There is then absolutely no chance of causing a sudden magnesium depletion.

Calcium is required for the nervous and muscular systems, normal heart function and blood coagulation. It is also needed for bone growth. However calcium must *always* be considered in conjunction with magnesium. The two minerals interact and must be kept in balance at all times. An excess of calcium will cause the balancing magnesium to be further depleted (which can be fatal), and vice versa.

It is unwise to feed calcium carbonate (ground limestone), di-calcium phosphate (DCP) or any other kind of straight calcium as these would cause a depletion of magnesium. DAP (di-ammonium phosphate) is occasionally recommended as a supplement, but it is even more dangerous because all three components deplete magnesium. When the latter is very high in the soil, the blood should be monitored to check if the levels are correct. When hand feeding, dolomite, which contains both minerals, should still be used. This is either because feed is frequently grown with artificial fertilisers like superphospate or some other form of phosphate, all of which tie up magnesium, or grown on soil that is inherently low in magnesium.

Some time ago, a headline in an English farming magazine read: 'Excess calcium gives cows mastitis'. This might just as easily have referred to horses. The statement is not strictly correct. Calcium does not cause mastitis, but depleting the magnesium needed to maintain udder health creates an imbalance, and mastitis organisms (variety immaterial) are then able to gain entry and proliferate.

Excess calcium in both the plant and animal world is linked with a weakening of the cell structure and lowering of immunity to disease, especially of viral origin.

Calcium will be found naturally in all feeds, and in lucerne in particular if it is well grown. This means dry land lucerne, grown without artificial fertilisers on remineralised soil. However, its presence depends on two factors:

> 1 That the original soil where the feed was grown con-
> tained adequate levels of calcium (and magnesium);
> and
>
> 2 Whether artificial fertilisers were used (these are
> heavily used in irrigation) — these reduce the levels of
> available minerals in the feed.

A lack of calcium causes conditions such as arthritis, uneven bone growth, knock knees, cow hocks, poor muscle tone leading to prolapses, poor teeth, general lack of wellbeing and a susceptibility to cold and therefore respiratory problems. Calcium and magnesium deficiencies will also cause lactation problems such as milk fever and mastitis. Researchers in the United States have also linked kidney stones with a lack of these essential minerals. For horses, calcium in these situations is best supplied in dolomite, even in districts where the magnesium is reasonably high. For prolapses and associated disorders, the best type of calcium to use is calcium fluoride — nothing to do with sodium fluoride — which is obtainable in the Cell Salts range from most chemists and health shops. This disorder is fairly rare, so the remedy is quite economical to use.

A soil analysis should be done wherever possible. In Australia, there are odd pockets where magnesium is higher than calcium, but they are rare. In the United States, it is the reverse; this is the reason why feed recommendations and supplements from the United States do not work here. It is important to remember that calcium (and magnesium) assimilation depends on adequate boron, copper and vitamins A and D in the diet. Vitamins A and D (found in cod-liver oil) should be available from sunlight and well-grown feed; otherwise they will have to be given as a drench or as an A and D (and usually E) injection.

Magnesium (Mg)

This mineral is found in dolomite and magnesite (the latter is known as keiserite in Europe and the United Kingdom). It is often expensive and is fairly rare, and is virtually fifty-fifty calcium and magnesium. For most practical purposes I shall refer to dolomite, as it is the most natural form of magnesium that is easily available. Epsom salts (magnesium sulphate) is another form, but this should only be used therapeutically in cases of sudden founder or some other condition — long-term administration damages the covering of the kidneys. It is quite often used as a soil dressing where the pH is high and the magnesium needs to be increased.

Magnesium orotate is another highly effective form now used for deficiency conditions like stringhalt; this is obtainable from a chemist or health store and is highly effective. It appears to have no side effects and can be used in conjunction with dolomite.

I went to see some friends at a big breed show in February 1998, but their vehicle had broken down on the way there. It was very hot and the horses had been on the road nine hours instead of their usual three to four hour journey. One of the horses was a stallion that they were going to show for another breeder and he had not been fed dolomite or any of the supplements I recommend. We went round to see the horse and he stood there with a light rug on which looked as though waves were rippling underneath it. His owners remarked on this and asked me what I thought. The horse had a bad case of travel tetany. Magnesium shortfalls always show up as trembling and shivering. I told them they would not be showing it tomorrow or any other day unless something was done soon, and told them to give it a few handfuls of feed with a tablespoon of dolomite in it. They did not have any at the show, but I had five magnesium orotate tablets in my bag, which I keep there for emergencies — heat stress can also bring about magnesium shortfalls in humans. I suggested to my friend that she crush up the five tablets (400 mg each, making 2000 mg in all, a small dose for a horse) and give them to the stallion in a handful of feed, hoping that it would be enough.

The horse had almost reached the stage of not wanting to eat; however, with a little persuasion I got the food into its mouth and I watched, looking at my watch to see how quickly the awful trembling would stop. It took between three and four minutes. I was impressed, but no one else was. I realised from the speed of the improvement that the magnesium had been absorbed through the membranes of the mouth. Dr Kristin Marriott, a vet with whom I have worked for several years, confirms this and tells me that she has, with equal success, used the rectal route.

Magnesium deficiency appears to be rapidly becoming the biggest problem in modern conventional farming worldwide, possibly even in the United States where it is almost universally high (except for a few well-defined areas like Florida and round the Ozarks). Certainly in the United Kingdom, magnesium deficiencies as we know them in Australia did not occur before artificial chemical fertilisers were in common use. Now they appear to be rife in livestock of all kinds. I was in the United Kingdom in the late 1990s and several jumping and flat-race trainers asked me questions about conditions that were not around in 1950 (when I worked in the industry).

Magnesium appears to be more readily inhibited than calcium by artificial fertilisers. Early experiments in this area by Peter Bennett indicated that two bags of superphospate were able to inhibit the uptake of 5 kg of magnesium to the hectare. Both magnesium and calcium are rendered inert in the body by sodium fluoride as used in our water supplies. This must be considered if horses are drinking water containing fluoride salts. Rain or bore water is better. Magnesium is needed for all enzymes in both the gut *and* in muscles to function correctly. I think this explains why so many animal keepers have told me that they felt dolomite had improved their feed conversion rate, as well as making mastitis and acetonaemia in milking animals a thing of the past. Most stock keepers consider minerals and vitamins, but the enzymes do not often figure.

Seventy per cent of ingested magnesium is needed for bone growth and the remaining thirty per cent is required for neuromuscular transmission, muscular health and a healthy nervous system. The section on calcium shows how magnesium can be depressed by an excess of calcium. It is also almost totally removed from the system by feeds high in nitrates, such as capeweed, variegated thistle and some broad-leaved plants. Horses grazing these must have dolomite added to their rations or they may get stringhalt — which is curable (on a good paddock) — or go blind, which seems to be irreversible.

Conditions caused by a deficiency of magnesium (with calcium) include grass, lactation and travel tetanies (see above); mastitis; arthritis; stringhalt; founder; warts (the virus that causes these prefers a magnesium deficient host); and uneven bone growth, as well as most of the conditions related to calcium deficiency.

Animals whose bones have shown abnormal growth patterns or changes have been much improved in a few months by supplementation of dolomite and the correct minerals. Bone plates which have not knit as they should are always due to a mineral imbalance; very rarely are they congenital (even then it can be due to the same cause, if the mare has been grazing capeweed or something similar).

It appears that it is seldom too late (or too early) to reverse mineral deficiencies by properly supplemented feeding. A client rang me, having bought a five-month-old thoroughbred colt with epiphysitis (open knees) so severe, the front legs were twisted round. She took it to a vet who said that a very expensive operation could cure it, but she decided to take it home and feed it properly instead (she already used my methods). Seven weeks later she loaded it into the trailer and took it down to the vet clinic. His reaction was to say, 'Thank goodness you got another horse!' The horse was completely normal.

Excessively nervous behaviour is also attributable to a lack of magnesium. Many animals have become much easier to manage when dolomite has been added to their rations, changing from excitable to quite calm individuals in a matter of hours or days. Any condition that involves trembling, shaking or excess excitability can nearly always be attributed to a lack of magnesium.

It should be remembered that overdosing with calcium and magnesium can lead to depletion of trace minerals and iodine. However, if oral copper poisoning is suspected, dolomite (with vitamin C) can be used quite successfully as an antidote (see copper section).

Magnesium should normally be obtained from feed grown in soils containing adequate levels of the mineral. Unfortunately, this is rarely the case, as most feed is grown using artificial fertilisers and/or on depleted land.

In Australia, there is another source of calcium and magnesium for those lucky enough to live in the right areas — the artesian bore. Analysing the water would be the best method of finding out what minerals a bore contains. They can vary immensely (even in the same district) and can also, sadly, be contaminated with spray and nitrate residues, as happens in America. I had hoped that this would not occur here, but reports of contamination have been common since the middle of the 1990s.

Dolomitic lime, if of a decent quality with a ratio of about 45 ppm calcium to 36 ppm magnesium, is the safest way of providing these minerals, whether in the feed or as a top dressing.

Plants that cause magnesium deficiencies in stock are capeweed (*arctotheca calendula*) and Smooth cat's ear (*hypochaeris glabra*). These plants can be taken as an indication of a sick paddock with low magnesium and usually calcium as well.

Cobalt (Co)

Cobalt is needed for healthy bone development and for the health of red blood cells. Cobalt anaemia causes persistent ill-thrift, depleted appetite, sub-normal temperature, susceptibility to cold and then death. This condition is sometimes referred to as a cobalt collapse. I did not think horses could be affected until someone rang in whose stallion in Queensland had the local vets completely bewildered. There were no actual clinical signs of illness except those mentioned. They had not taken its temperature either. Unfortunately this condition is not generally understood these days.

The signs of a cobalt collapse are insidious: a slight lowering in appetite and unwillingness to move around. The droppings become progressively looser and the horse can still look a million dollars! The temperature seeems to be the only indication other than death, which usually occurs within seventy to eighty hours. Years ago, I had just won best exhibit at a show with a goat already sold interstate. She came into milking the next morning with all the symptoms mentioned above plus lowered milk yield. I loaded her into the Kombi and took her to the University of Melbourne clinical centre straight away. The chief vet praised her appearance and fetched in the other vets to see 'this magnificent animal'. I suggested rather acidly that they take her temperature, as her ears were cold. It was three degrees below normal. The response was, 'it's not significant, take her home'. I did, then stuck my nose into the book we all learnt from (*Goat Husbandry* by Dr David Mackenzie) and gave the goat a B12 injection. It recovered immediately. I always had to write a thesis for the University if I had something new — this was a mini-thesis. I heard that after that episode, if anything came in off-colour, it got its B12 injection!

The first sign of a cobalt shortfall is unhappiness, followed by lack of appetite, scouring, wasting and death in about seventy to eighty hours if nothing is done. For the initial diagnosis, an animal's temperature should be taken if it seems to be off-colour. If it is short of cobalt, it will be sub-normal. Vitamin B12 injections (*not* orally, 10 ml) will bring about a dramatic recovery, and these days we give 10 ml of VAM (vitamins, minerals and amino acids in liquid form) as well. This highlights the importance of having the soil analysed. Cobalt deficiency is caused by a low pH acidity which inhibits the presence of the mineral and overuse of artificial fertilisers. I think it is uncommon to find an original deficiency (except for areas in western Victoria and eastern South Australia). On one very poor farm with all these conditions, the cobalt was back in the food chain in about fifteen months after analysing and top-dressing the soil with two tonnes of dolomite to the hectare as recommended by the analyst.

Cobalt is synthesised into vitamin B12 in the gut (as is iron), and this synthesis can cease to work in cases of extra stress, illness or the administration of drugs. When this happens, the only way to reactivate the synthesis is to *inject* vitamin B12; orally it will *not* work. It is *most* important that this injection is *always* given when antibiotics are used. This is a water-soluble injection which is completely safe; the body merely excretes any administered surplus to requirements.

Vitamin B12 is a great help in encouraging all ages to eat after illness or stress, and should in fact be given as a routine measure on these occasions. It should also be given as a matter of course to mares that have had a rough time foaling, to help them get back onto their food. Weakly foals often respond to a 10 ml injection too.

Cobalt sulphate is extremely toxic (and expensive) and should only be given at a rate of 3 g between ten horses per day. Extra amounts of cobalt sulphate should only be prescribed by a vet.

Feeding seaweed meal by making it freely available will help, because seaweed contains all minerals in natural form. It is often enough to correct any problems. If the land is cobalt deficient, the best course is to have this amended by remineralising (see this and previous chapters) with the required lime minerals. Copper deficiencies are serious, but far more so if cobalt is also missing.

Copper (Cu)

This is a mineral that can be top-dressed in areas where copper deficiencies are a big problem and the pH is around 7.0 to 8.0. A printout in *Acres USA* some years ago told of farmers beyond Goyders Lagoon in northern South Australia in the 1940s, who had sheep which had become virtually unproductive due to what we now know are deficiencies of copper. This affected the wool and also caused a lack of oestrus. The farmers spread copper sulphate over their property and, as it is a high pH area, the operation was a success. In late 2001, I worked in this region with farmers and it was obvious that mineral deficiencies were becoming a problem again, as the sheep were really punishing the salt bush in their attempts to find what they needed.

Neal Kinsey says that rust in crops only occurs on copper-deficient soils. Again, it is a case of needing to pull the soil back into the correct balance so that the copper is available. Feed made from rusty crops can cause ill health to all stock, including horses. As I write, baled silage is causing cattle deaths due to photo-sensitisation in Gippsland in Victoria. Presumably the above conditions apply wherever this silage was grown.

Copper in the soil is inhibited when the pH is either too low or too high, and the latter effect is worse in droughts. When I was investigating why copper shortfalls were so great, a researcher at Monash University studying the mineral told me that copper is inhibited virtually one hundred per cent by superphosphate, so putting it out with copper is not an option. Getting the soil into balance is.

> NOTE: Andre Voisin's Soil, Grass and Cancer confirms the above and adds that all nitrogenous fertilisers (urea, ammonium nitrate) totally suppress the uptake of copper — he states that a hundred per cent is lost. Eve Balfour (the Haughley Experiment) observed the same thing when superphosphate was used. Both Balfour and Voisin's work took place in the 1950s!

There are three so-called weeds that carry copper in amounts large enough to kill light-coloured stock if they are driven to eating them by hunger. The dark-coloured animals on the other hand, do very well! St John's Wort (*hypericum*) and Paterson's curse (*echium plantagineum*) are both deep-rooted plants that grow in copper-deficient topsoil, and are probably nature's answer to replacing copper near the surface. The third plant, heliotrope (*Heliotropium amplexicaule*), is a shallow-rooted annual that grows in soils low in calcium and magnesium but containing adequate copper. It causes stock to die of jaundice like the other two, and deaths from all three can be stopped if the stock have licks containing dolomite available.

A horse's body needs copper for optimum health and resistance to disease, especially diseases of fungal origin which include protozoal-type infestations. The immune system needs copper to operate correctly. Internal parasites are only found in horses that are deficient in the mineral. Failure to come into oestrus regularly is possibly the worst effect of an animal having low levels of copper from a financial point of view. Mares whose copper levels are right, cycle regularly at the correct time. Horses that are half in-season can often be turned round in twenty-four hours or less by 10 ml of VAM.

Anaemia, poor coat colour, cancer, Crohn's disease, proud flesh, ringworm, mud fever, herpes-related conditions, seedy toe, onychomycosis (white line disease or canker), worms, wind sucking, fence eating and many more conditions all result when copper levels are low. This includes brucellosis, tuberculosis and, as mentioned, protozoal conditions — especially when linked with deficiencies of iodine, manganese and cobalt. Dark animals that are off-colour (literally) are suffering from lack of copper.

Perhaps the most serious effect of a copper shortfall is anaemia, especially in Australia where most soils have adequate iron. Without copper, iron cannot be assimilated. Given the fact that iron tonics are undesirable at the best of times, seeing that horses get the correct amount of copper in their rations is the obvious answer. Do not be led astray by the enormous amounts of iron tonics offered on sale in fodder stores; they do not deal with the cause of the anaemia and inhibit vitamin E.

For paddock and range-fed horses there is a lick the farmer can make up which is totally balanced. This is not to be added to working horse rations — feed them as suggested in chapter seven.

    25 kg of dolomite
    4 kg of copper sulphate
    4 kg of milling sulphur
    4 kg of seaweed meal (urea free)

This lick must be put out in a *rainproof* container.

Research carried out in Japan in the 1960s on humans established that black-haired people needed nearly six times more copper than fair-haired ones, and I have also found these ratios to be right for dark and light-coloured horses. It will be noticed that dark horses often suffer from the deficiency conditions mentioned above before their lighter-coloured counterparts. However, horses also seem to be governed by the colour of their skins, and in the copper-deficiency disease stakes, chestnuts, blacks and buckskins are neck and neck!

Horses whose coats are staring or looking rough and fluffy in winter — or indeed any other time — are always short on copper (even Shetland ponies and donkeys!). If the hair is examined closely, a little curl will be seen at the end — another sure sign of copper deficiency. In black horses, a red to rusty sheen on the coat is from the same cause. Many of these conditions can also be occasioned by bad worm infestations as well (which only occur when copper is inadequate).

In Thomas Hungerford's book, *Diseases of Livestock*, he says that repeated and unexplained scouring is often caused by a lack of copper. I have also found this to be so. Occasionally, stock will show the classic 'spectacles' appearance when copper deficient. The skin round the eyes appears light-coloured and pulled away, making the animal look as though it is wearing spectacles.

Copper is highly toxic in excess and does not taste nice to humans at all, although I have spoken to a number of people (of very fine physique) who regularly had it given to them as children (in cod-liver oil). I have also known of animals and birds who willingly ate it when they were badly deficient. The horse's tolerance seems to be fairly high and cases of copper poisoning will not occur if supplementation is carefully monitored. One fact should be remembered: feed that is too high in protein can raise the requirement for copper quite materially.

Zinc in excess suppresses copper. The reverse has now been proven not to be true, although we were told for many years that it was.

Too much copper kills, but too little does just the same. Copper injections should be avoided because an overdose cannot be treated. If too much copper is administered orally, dolomite, and sodium ascorbate vitamin C powder (orally) with vitamin B15 injections produce a very quick cure. Copper toxicity shows up as an acute liver attack. I tried this once when I purposely fed a pale-coloured poddy calf an excessive dose — it recovered in twenty minutes using the above method. *Only* copper sulphate should be fed to horses (or any other stock), never copper carbonate. Copper carbonate is twice as strong as copper sulphate in the body and is not easily lost like a sulphate. An overdose could be fatal.

At the request of a copper researcher, I fed copper carbonate to my horses and goats for four months, carefully halving the amounts I would usually feed. The exercise was not a success. Both horses and goats did much better on the sulphate variety of copper — and there is at least room for error if there was an overdose. There is no margin for error with the carbonate.

Seaweed meal contains a significant amount of copper and providing the meal often helps to offset shortfalls.

The University of Minnesota researched copper levels and ponies some years ago (the paper is listed in the Bibliography). It proved that equines apparently have either an astonishing tolerance to copper or more likely a very large requirement. They started feeding copper to a group of ponies, determined to kill them and then reduce the amounts of copper until they came down to a safe level. None died, they just looked better and better, and they concluded as above.

For those who are firm in their belief that copper sulphate is dangerous, the following anecdote may set their minds at rest. I was consulted by a complete stranger — a trainer of gallopers — whose horses had a bad case of copper poisoning. She had taken five gallopers on a 'raid' to the southern states and hired a barn for them instead of loose boxes. She left a drum of molass water (she has learnt about that now) for them at night. No one had noticed that above the drum there was a high shelf with a container on it, holding at least a kilogram of copper sulphate. A cat knocked it into the bucket one night. For some reason, the mixture was very attractive to the horses and they drank the lot — which they would not usually do. They were five *very* sick horses, but the trainer did a great job and kept them on their feet. Her vet, an American, was terrific and we discussed the treatment. Thank goodness she was a confirmed user of vitamin B15 (DADA), so 12 ml of that daily was prescribed, as well as intravenous vitamin C. Also, sodium ascorbate and dolomite (a tablespoon of each at a time) were administered two or three times a day when possible, and activated charcoal was added to that mixture.

The bilirubin count went up to eighty (it should have been seven) and I was beginning to wonder if we would win, when it all fell into place. They were back in training on the fifth day — none the worse for their binge! Top marks to both trainer and vet.

Iodine

It seems that the whole of Australia is iodine deficient, surprisingly even in coastal areas. In a small country such as the United Kingdom, the Atlantic winds used to keep the iodine levels up, and usually continental coastal areas have good levels. However, none of these rules seem to apply any longer, and it seems that extended use of high analysis artificial fertilisers has affected iodine availability everywhere.

Iodine is not truly a mineral and thus cannot figure on an analysis. It is *essential* however for the health of the thyroid gland, which controls the health of all the glands in the whole body. No thyroid, no life. Therefore, if an animal is iodine deficient, no matter what feed or minerals or vitamins are given, they will not be assimilated properly until the iodine requirements are met. Fortunately, the requirement is not very high, and access to the lick described earlier or feeding seaweed meal on demand is usually quite enough to meet it. It has saved many a horse!

This is preferable to using inorganic iodine in the form of potassium iodide or Lugol's solution as we used to have to do before seaweed meal became available. Both are very toxic in excess as well as being expensive, and Lugol's now appears to be unobtainable (although I note that it is still used in the United Kingdom). A vet will advise on alternate forms of iodine supplementation if necessary.

If there is an iodine shortfall, obviously the animal's system cannot function properly. This should be considered as the basis of any problem. As seaweed supplementation now has become the norm in all stock feeding worldwide, deficiencies should be unlikely. Seaweed provides a huge spectrum of minerals in their most natural and assimilable form.

Signs of an iodine deficiency are, in severe cases, a swollen goitre and, in its mild form, dandruff or scurf, and of course sub-normal health. It *must* be remembered that the signs of iodine excess and deficiency are identical, so if a horse shows any of these signs, make seaweed meal available. Animals will not touch it if they have too much in their systems already. Putting it in feed could lead to severe trouble. *Do not ever* do so.

> NOTE: *The thyroid gland is a hard protuberance in the middle of the throat. Swelling at the side of the throat always indicates infected or sore salivary glands. These should usually feel soft.*

A potent and common cause of iodine deficiency is the overfeeding of legumes such as lucerne, clovers, beans, peas, soya products, lucerne trees (tagasaste) and lupins. These are termed *goitragenic* feeds, because in extreme cases they cause the thyroid to swell. Feeding too many legumes will cause a preponderance of male offspring. The female foetus has the greatest need for iodine. If there is a deficiency, she does not develop and is probably reabsorbed. It is also possible in some cases that females are not even conceived for this reason. Occasionally, in iodine-deficient animals having multiple births, the males are born strong, but the females are born weak, dying and hairless.

Feeds high in nitrates such as capeweed and many broad-leaved species, even clover on occasion when present in large amounts (such as after a drought), can also inhibit iodine and cause thyroid disfunction. If horses are on paddocks largely growing capeweed, iodine supplementation is necessary as well as dolomite. Better still, get them off the paddock! (See the magnesium section.) Again, seaweed meal would usually be enough, but horses should not be pastured in those conditions.

Remember that an iodine deficiency should always be considered as the base cause of practically every problem. A blood test will identify a large iodine deficiency, but might not highlight a chronic shortfall.

Iron (Fe)

In many soils in Australia, iron is fairly plentiful or over-supplied, partly due to the volcanic origin of much of the country. It is also often the only mineral left after extended use of artificial fertilisers. A Gippsland farm with iron that was 1600 times too high and salt that was 600 times too high found that they partly inhibited everything else. Potassium and vitamin E are the major casualties, as a rule. Iron destroys the latter in the body; this is why iron tonics must be avoided as far as possible. This situation can be altered quite easily by top-dressing the area after a soil analysis. Bringing the calcium/magnesium/gypsum up to the correct level is usually all that is needed to balance out the iron and salt that is too high.

The most important fact to remember about iron in relation to horses (and all life) is that without copper it *cannot* be assimilated. Many so-called iron deficiencies are merely due to a copper shortfall. Iron is necessary for the health of red blood cells and therefore is necessary for the horse's general wellbeing.

As mentioned in the section on copper, in spite of the prevalence of iron, anaemia is one of the biggest causes of sickness in stock. Giving daily injections of vitamin B12 (10 ml at a time) while introducing the correct amount of copper to the diet is preferable to iron tonics, which may be used *only* as a short-term remedy for a few days. Copper supplementation will raise iron levels very quickly and does not have the great disadvantage of totally suppressing vitamin E, unlike dosing with inorganic iron.

If there is a lack of iron in the paddocks, top-dressing with basic slag, a by-product of the iron smelting industry, was the old way of amending a shortfall. This practice was quite usual in Europe and America, and was generally done every six to ten years by conventional farmers. Organic farmers do not use it now. However, I am yet to see an analysis in Australia that showed a serious lack of iron, although this does quite often occur in the United Kingdom.

Manganese (Mn)

This mineral is an antagonist of copper, and by destroying that mineral in the brain causes conditions akin to BSE and possibly its variants as well. Mark Purdey, a self-taught bio-chemist and dairy farmer in the southern part of the United Kingdom, has linked an excess of manganese to BSE and its variants. He found that people whose diets had more that 30 or 40 ppm manganese in Slovakia were at risk of contracting and often had BSE. On a soil analysis, the desired level is approximately 20 ppm. A pour-on called pthalimido-phosphorus is also implicated in this condition.

When I was learning about farming and soils in the United Kingdom, we were taught that manganese and molybdenum were best left alone as they would find their desired level once the soils were fully balanced.

Molybdenum (Mo)

This element is needed for maximum fertility. A deficiency can occur in land that is exhausted and low in organic mat-ter, especially if the pH is below 5.0. However, high levels of the mineral are dangerous and can be an indirect cause of anaemia (by affecting copper and cobalt utilisation).

This is probably the reason why we were taught to adjust the levels of the other elements through top-dressing and raising the lime minerals to their correct level, rather than altering the molybdenum. Increasing the organic matter in the soil is the best remedy.

It should be noted that there are areas in Victoria where the molybdenum levels are rising due to fallout from some of the industrial complexes. The vets who first drew my attention to this about fifteen years ago were extremely worried about the situation. Some coal farm and garden products have been dangerously high in molybdenum from that source — always check. Given its role in tying up copper, this could be serious. One ppm is usually all that is needed of this mineral.

Phosphorus (P)

This mineral is essential for healthy growth and life, and should be kept in balance with calcium and magnesium. An excess will lead to bone fragility and many other problems of the kind associated with calcium and magnesium deficiencies.

Phosphorus will not be lacking in healthy soils where organic matter and humus are in balance. Soils that have been heavily cropped with nothing returned to the soil will eventually be lacking in organic matter and available phosphorus. But even those soils have a locked up phosphorus bank as shown in chapter two.

Phosphorus deficiencies in horses appear to be fairly rare even when levels are extremely low. If they all have access to the minerals they need, either in licks, in feed and/or free choice seaweed meal, the horses do not seem to have this problem.

Potassium (K), potash

Potassium is absolutely essential for all life, both plant and animal. It is rapidly being depleted due to chemical farming. The Haughley experiment in the United Kingdom proved that potash was the mineral most affected by artificial fertilisers and showed that, in spite of being replaced with muriate or sulphate (of potash), it was quite steadily lost. On land that was being farmed naturally it was found to be self renewing with no danger of running out. On poor, low pH soils, potassium is often inhibited by high iron as well as acidity.

According to Charlotte Auerbach's book, *The Science of Genetics*, a lack of potassium and vitamin C at conception can interfere with the true pattern of genetic inheritance. When breeding valuable horses, it is therefore essential that the paddocks be as healthy as possible. The most serious result of a potassium deficiency is difficult births (dystokia). Having to pull every foal is *not* desirable. In the short-term, cider vinegar contains enough potassium to enable all horses to have their foals naturally, but raising the health of the paddocks is the best long-term solution. I remember a vet from the western district of Victoria telling me that in the 1965 drought he had to pull ninety-five per cent of all the calves in his area. There was no greenfeed and he concluded that a potassium deficiency was the cause. We now know that he was right.

A potassium deficiency causes constriction of the blood vessels in areas of the body where they are fairly fine, hence navicular disease that occurs in horses and RSI occurring in humans. Both of these respond to potassium supplementation either by tablets or extra cider vinegar. Dystokia seems to be caused by a lack of blood supply to the uterus and cervix in the final stages of pregnancy. In a normal, healthy pregnancy, the foetus moves constantly until it is presented in the birth canal in the appropriate position. Birth should then take place without problems. When potassium is lacking, the foetus is locked in position and (speaking as one who has pulled an inordinate number of calves, lambs and one foal, all for other people) it is virtually immovable! This is very damaging to both mare and foal.

Sodium also plays a role relative to potassium. Check the entry on sodium.

Selenium (Se)

It is doubtful whether a deficiency of selenium affects plant growth very materially. Possibly it does not figure on many soil analyses for this reason. However, there is absolutely no doubt that a shortfall can affect horses and other animals very seriously indeed, and can cause death in a great many instances.

When we first came to Australia in the late 1950s, selenium deficiencies were only believed to occur in parts of the western district of Victoria and round Canterbury in New Zealand. However, as time went on, rumours of selenium shortfalls in plenty of other places started to come in. In the mid 1980s, a rather cross vet friend in Gippsland asked me to find out what I could about the mineral, as he was sure many of the animals in his practice were suffering quite severely from a deficiency. He had been categorically told by the Department of Agriculture that it was impossible, as there was no record of a lack of selenium in that part of Australia (they were correct). After some research and an increased knowledge of what low pH and artifical fertilisers were doing to minerals, the rest of the information fell into place.

We were faced with a picture showing that a whole host

of minerals were being tied up and rendered unavailable by artificial fertilisers with or without low pH. Selenium in particular was at great risk, because the sulphur levels in all soils were falling dramatically for the same reason.

When I started keeping stock in Australia in 1960, I was told that all goats needed a teaspoon of sulphur a week and horses needed a dessertspoon. This was to keep lice at bay. Apparently no one knew that it was also required for the amino acids in the gut. Within ten years that ration had become once a *day* for the same purpose, and now it is advisable to give horses a tablespoon daily. Warding off exterior parasites is only part of the function of sulphur. Its amino acids are needed to assimilate selenium — which is even more important. This was the information that the vets needed and it explained why selenium deficiencies had become so widespread. Not only was the selenium tied up, so was the sulphur that was needed for its assimilation (see also chapter one).

Like most trace minerals, selenium is equally dangerous in excess or deficiency. A small amount is needed for fertility, particularly in stallions. Without it, the sperm tend to be weak and drop their tails. The mineral is also needed for healthy muscles. White muscle disease and muscular dystrophy are both conditions exacerbated by a shortage of selenium. Complete and sudden cessation of growth, with or without signs of muscle wasting, could be a sign of selenium deficiency in young animals.

Excess selenium can cause a malformed foetus and/or poisoning. Sodium selenite (inorganic selenium) is only obtainable from a veterinary surgeon, so accidental poisonings should not occur. However, 1 mg of organic selenium (as in seaweed meal) is equal to 4 mg of inorganic selenium. Seaweed is therefore the best method of supplementation.

Selenium is linked with vitamin E and often giving

vitamin E alone will effect a cure in mild cases of deficiency. In fact, this can be used as a test. If a sick animal (weighing around 60 kg) responds to 2000 units of vitamin E, you can be sure that it is suffering from a selenium deficiency.

Sodium (Na)

Sodium must be in balance with potassium in the soil, but all too often it is in excess, especially if sodic fertilisers like artificial potash have been used. In some parts of Australia it is naturally high unless very careful farming methods are used.

Salt is essential for life, but in our civilisation there is generally far too much already in the food chain. In excess, salt depresses potassium, and causes oedema (fluid retention), cancer and other degenerative conditions. Excess sodium also prevents the horse from using its fodder correctly. However, when animals have a craving for salt and eat large quantities of it, they are frequently looking for potassium, as the two interchange in the body. A farmer rang me to complain that his sheep (on a very poor farm) were eating salt by the bag. I suggested that he obtain some cider vinegar and spray their hay with it once or twice a week. The salt consumption stopped within days. This could easily happen with horses.

There is generally enough salt for normal requirements in feeds. Animals needing extra are short of other minerals. Adding seaweed, or putting it out in the licks is the best option, but it is also a good idea to have a block of real rock salt available in all the horse paddocks. Do not buy made-up purified salt blocks. Stick to the most basic form possible.

Years ago, a doctor told me about troops in the tropics who were always given salt tablets, as it was thought to be a necessity. It was discovered that when their diets were amended to contain more essential minerals, the demand for salt dropped off considerably. I also observed this in my animals that received their required minerals. They hardly, if ever, touched the salt on offer. But when a new horse or goat arrived, it often spent the first few days punishing the salt blocks. However once the minerals from the feed came into play, they, like the others, ignored the salt.

Sulphur (S)

The first book on this mineral is a booklet put out by the CSIR (no O in those days) in 1928 called *The Utilisation of Sulphur by Animals*. Keratin, a very important constituent of wool, hair, hooves and horns, depends on the cysteine in sulphur as well as adequate copper. It is only one of the many amino acids in the mineral. Protein levels in plants depend on amino acids of sulphur, which may perhaps explain the falling proteins in crops as the sulphur in the soil runs out. Logically it could be expected that the sulphuric acid used in the manufacture of superphosphate would mean a plentiful supply of sulphur, but the reverse appears to be the case.

It is now fashionable to say that our knowledge of sulphur is fairly recent, but the CSIR booklet from 1928 lists all the amino acids of sulphur. In the past, horse owners have recognised its importance, and it is often mentioned in old veterinary and cavalry manuals. On the land, gypsum (calcium sulphate) is generally used to raise sulphur levels where both calcium and sulphur are needed, straight sulphur is used otherwise.

CSIRO later published a short article on sulphur in their *Rural Research Bulletin*, No. 22, in the 1960s, and they found that without sulphur's amino acids, stock did not do well. They did not mention the onset of exterior parasites and may not have linked the two. They established that as far as oral administration was concerned, as long as the sulphur does not exceed two per cent of all fodder taken in the day, it was quite safe. This is a very high margin.

Animals that are sulphur deficient may have lice or other exterior parasites. They will not digest their feed properly because they are deficient in essential amino acids, especially cysteine and methionine. Young horses will not progress as well as they should if sulphur is missing. The mineral is often beneficial for skin ailments, both topically (when applied to the skin) and added to the feed. Skin problems, therefore, could be another sign of sulphur deficiency.

Sulphur can be added to feeds at any stage of a horse's development. For lice infestation, a heaped tablespoon every day will be necessary. A flat tablespoon per horse, mixed in the feed daily, is all that is needed for maintenance. It also helps to rub in sulphur down the infested horse's back-line.

Zinc (Zn)

Zinc is usually fairly well supplied in soil, but is now being listed as a possible casualty of artificial fertilisers (along with other trace minerals). This was not originally considered a possibility.

Zinc levels that are too high can depress copper and this often occurs. The reverse of this used to be believed, but does not seem to be true. Certainly, the tests I have done with stock with very high levels of copper indeed made no difference to their zinc requirements.

Zinc is necessary for healthy reproductive systems in both males and females, particularly the former, as the prostate gland has a high zinc requirement. However, it is probable that there is not much difference between the requirements of the female reproductive system and the male. The prostate problems are merely more obvious.

Eczema responds very quickly to extra zinc, which can be given in the form of seaweed meal or by feeding zinc sulphate. Zinc sulphate can be used for supplementation. As it is also one of the most plentiful minerals found in seaweed, often giving seaweed meal in licks or freely is enough to meet the zinc requirements of most animals. This form of zinc is apparently more effective than using the sulphate, as are most minerals in their natural form. When sheep being shipped to the Middle East were dying soon after the boats left, it was discovered that it was due to a zinc/potassium shortfall. This was not remedied until seaweed was used as an additive. The initial extra amounts of straight zinc and potassium added to the pellets had failed to remedy the situation, but the small amount supplied in the natural seaweed meal was able to work best.

Zinc is also indicated where recovery from sickness is not as fast as it should be. Again, seaweed products will probably be all that are needed.

> NOTE: Herpes rhinovirus (the source of cold sores and foot and mouth disease) is linked to a lack of zinc. So is Crohn's disease (and Johne's disease in livestock).

Buying minerals and vitamins

It is useful to know that sulphur is the yellow powder that used to be called 'flowers of sulphur' and is now marketed as milling sulphur for orchard use. Copper sulphate is popularly known as 'bluestone' in many country places and is listed as being around twenty-seven per cent copper, as a rule. Dolomite is a crushed rock mined in that form containing calcium and magnesium, not as is occasionally tried, a made-up mixture of lime and epsom salts, which does not work as well!

NOTE: *Lugol's solution is made as follows: five per cent iodine; ten per cent potassium; eighty-five per cent rainwater. (Many chemists no longer have this recipe.)*

5 Vitamins — Minerals come first!

If an animal's intake of minerals is in total balance, vitamin deficiencies should not occur. The title of this chapter is quoted freely from the work of Dr Joel Wallach and emphasises the fact that without the necessary minerals in the pasture and feed, vitamins cannot perform as they should. Behind every vitamin deficiency there is a mineral one. Note that all vitamins are destroyed by light and should only be purchased in opaque containers.

> NOTE: *Liquid paraffin should never be given internally to any animal, as it destroys vitamins in the gut. If oil is needed, it is best to use a cooking variety. This was drummed into me in the late forties and fifties when I worked helping local vets in the United Kingdom, and it still applies.*

Vitamin A (retinol) and vitamin D (cholecalciferol)

For practical purposes, these vitamins should always be considered together. Generally they are found together in nature. Vitamins A and D in fish-liver oils are in the correct natural proportions. They are also found in mutton bird oil. However, given the incidence of BSE, I am loath to suggest feeding anything except fish products. Both vitamins A and D on their own can be dangerous if used in excess. They are fat-soluble vitamins and so share with vitamin E and K the property of not being lost in the body as easily as those that are water-soluble.

Vitamin A, retinol

Vitamin A is normally stored in the liver in amounts high enough to enable a horse to cope with a prolonged period on dry feed — for approximately three to five months — but in a drought which exceeds that time, deficiencies will start to develop.

Mares that are low in vitamin A will not hold to service, or the foetus will be absorbed soon after. They will also be at risk of abortion and/or uterine and vaginal ill health. Stallions will tend to get stones in their urethra and will go permanently infertile if the deficiency is serious. Should a mare be deficient in vitamin A when she foals, the foal may not live beyond nine days, as it will not receive enough vitamin A from the mare to last till the vitamin A in the mare's milk takes over. There is also the distinct possibility that the foal will be born with contracted tendons (knuckle-over). However, this is very quickly reversed with 8–10 ml of cod-liver oil. Giving this orally for two days should be enough (see chapter eight).

Breeding mares must have feed rich in vitamin A prior to foaling. Running them on a chemical-free, remineralised, green paddock can be enough to raise vitamin A levels. If there is any doubt about their vitamin A and D levels, mares should be given 20 ml each a week in their feed coming up to foaling.

Vitamin A is particularly important for the health of the eyes, and an outbreak of pinkeye (conjunctivitis) is a sure sign of a deficiency, as are worm infestations. A harsh, dry coat and runny eyes (both signs of worms and a copper deficiency) can also be a sign of vitamin A shortfall.

A further cause of depleted vitamin A has recently been reported at length in *Acres USA*: overhead power lines. This backs up my own findings for goats reared under the main grid (I leased them unaware of this fact). They appeared to have lost the ability to synthesise their own vitamin A. For three years after leaving the locality, these goats needed ongoing vitamin A supplementation, no matter how good the season.

Another factor that can affect vitamin A levels is processes where hormones are used, such as embryo transplants and similar procedures. Horses which are being used for this purpose should receive vitamin A (and D) regularly, or they may abort and waste the whole process.

Vitamin A is also susceptible to light. If a horse is left in light for twenty-four hours, its vitamin A reserves will be severely depleted. A period of darkness is needed to preserve the normal functioning of the vitamin. If using a water-soluble vitamin A and D emulsion, do not add it to the water or the vitamins will be destroyed by the light. Vitamin A is better if it is given by a drench or included in the feed where it will be eaten straight away. If grass hay has no green colour at all, one can safely assume it will not have any vitamin A either.

Supplementation can be by cod-liver oil, or A, D and E powder, emulsion or injections. A and D injections can occasionally cause trouble at the site of the injection due to the oily nature of the fluid, so it is probably better given orally. The powder (sometimes difficult to obtain) is usually quite palatable and can be mixed with the feed, as can the emulsion or oil. Of course, the best method of supplementing with vitamin A would be by giving chemical-free, well-grown and harvested greenfeed. There have been cases where conjunctivitis has been cured by merely moving afflicted stock to a paddock of properly-grown greenfeed.

Vitamin D, cholecalciferol

This vitamin is needed for bone growth and the absorption of calcium. If it is missing, bone deformities will occur. No matter how much dolomite is added to the ration, without vitamin (A and) D, the calcium and magnesium are not correctly utilised. Signs of vitamin D deficiency are unnatural bone formations and, in mild forms, a very harsh coat. Like vitamin A, this vitamin should be found in all properly-grown greenfeed, but the chief source of supply is sunlight, from which it is synthesised on the skin. This is an argument against rugging a horse excessively, except when the weather is very cold. A horse can absorb much of the vitamin D it needs through its head and neck, but the food source is also needed. Rugs that cover the entire body are *not* desirable in summer. Properly fed horses do not lose their coat colour (see the section on copper).

Vitamin B complex

This covers a whole range of vitamins: B1, B2, B3, B5, B6, B12, B15 and biotin. Even now, new ones are being added as the knowledge of this field increases. In 1982, PABA was removed from the list and renamed vitamin H. These B vitamins should normally be present in all well-grown feeds, especially grains, but they may be missing if the soils from which the feed came were deficient in magnesium or cobalt — which happens frequently. Milling and irradiation destroys most B and other vitamins.

In theory, all the B vitamins are present in vitamin B complex powders or injections, but in practice this is not effective and it is wiser to give the specific vitamins that are needed for best results. B vitamins are found in fresh, unmilled grains or fodder; barley, for example, contains the incredibly important vitamin B5.

VAM, made by Naturevet, consists of vitamins, amino acids and minerals in liquid form, and is an excellent and very effective source. 10 ml by injection for horses is the best pick-up I know, and Naturevet now produce an oral paste that is nearly as effective.

Vitamin B1, thiamine

Until a few years ago, this vitamin was hardly considered in either human or animal health; if it was, the requirement was thought to be insignificant. Now we know that it is absolutely essential and deficiencies are far more common than had previously been supposed. They are caused by feed too high in carbohydrates (a rare effect) and fungal poisoning — only too common nowadays. Deficiency signs vary from photosensitisation and mild distress to staggering, lateral incoordination and blindness, followed by death in about seventy-two hours. An animal deficient in this and other B vitamins often shows scarlet streaking in the membranes of the mouth; in rare cases, *all* the gums are bright scarlet (see section on colitis X).

Thiamine is destroyed by thiaminase which is present in some moulds, so feed suspected of being mouldy should *never* be fed to any horse. Unfortunately, these moulds survive the process of being made into mixed feeds and pelletising. If treatment is not started immediately, death can follow in a day or two, and thiamine is only effective against one kind of mould. It should be noted that these conditions only appear on pastures that are extremely poor and out of balance.

The moulds start in the soil organisms because the ground is so sick; they then affect the plants and the horse eating the pasture or its products. Diseases caused by moulds are serious and often cause residual damage even if they can be cured. This is one sound reason for only feeding mixtures that you have made up yourself. You can see if the ingredients are mouldy, which you cannot when they are pelletised (see section on botulism in chapter eight).

B1, like most B injections, is water-soluble. This means that any excess is eliminated by the body, and there is not the danger of overdosing as there could be with an oil-based injection. The dose recommended for this condition is approximately 8 mcg of injectable vitamin B1 (obtainable from any vet or feed store) per kilogram of bodyweight, intramuscularly, every six hours until the signs disappear. One millilitre of injectable vitamin B1 should contain 126 mg — consult the bottle.

Note that thiaminase poisoning is one of over two hundred diseases caused by moulds, and vitamin B1 may not always work. Sometimes a massive dose of vitamin C may help, but residual hormonal damage can be the result, according to Dr Alenson DVM. Prevention is definitely better than cure.

Vitamin B2, riboflavin

This vitamin would normally be present in well-grown green-feed, and is needed for the health of the mouth and lips and for the eye's ability to withstand bright lights. Cataract is sometimes caused by a deficiency. It is also needed in digestion. Deficiency signs could be cracks round the mouth, and a bright magenta colour in the tongue or gums. Difficulty in urinating has also been noted in animals deficient in this vitamin.

Supplementation can be by crushed tablets, but a supply of really well-grown greenfeed should set right a deficiency fairly quickly.

Vitamin B3, niacin, niacinimide, nicotinamide or nicotinic acid

Any of the above names are used to describe this vitamin, which has only recently been called vitamin B3.

A deficiency is associated with mental trauma like forgetfulness and senility, neither of which should affect horses. Barley is also one of the best sources of this vitamin.

Vitamin B5, panthonic acid, calcium pantenthonate

This vitamin plays a crucial part in a horse's resistance to disease, because it is needed — along with vitamin C — for manufacturing cortisone in the adrenal cortex. Any horse that is very ill could be in need of both vitamins. This is why giving vitamin C for any illness is so helpful. The treatment of any illness caused by an infection should include extra vitamin C, and when grain is fed, barley (soaked, but not boiled as that destroys the vitamins) should also be fed. In the old days, barley water was given to sick humans and would also help horses that were too sick to be given grain. It was made by soaking barley and retaining the water.

In one example, pigs in the United Kingdom whose barley was replaced by maize (which provided vitamin B6) suffered from pantothenic acid (B5) deficiency, causing ill-thrift, paralysis and death. On post mortem, the symptoms resembled necrotic enteritis. Once the barley was added to the diet again there was no more trouble. This phenomenon was also noted in pigs fed maize with meat meal, linseed meal and lucerne. Rather than administer artificial cortisone, it is therefore best to feed the required grain and healthy green-feed so the horse makes its own. On one occasion, a trainer in the United Kingdom was warned off by racing authorities about using cortisone, but it was proven that his horse's mech-anism for making its own was the cause of the positive swab! Injections of B5 are also sometimes obtainable. Instructions on the bottle should be followed. Like other B vitamins, it is found in well-grown greenfeed and barley grain. Half a tea-spoon of turmeric two or three times a week appears to be sufficient to maintain B5 levels, as well as barley. It is useful in situations where it is not practical to use barley grain.

Vitamin B6, pyridoxine

This B vitamin is needed for resistance to infections, partic-ularly herpes types. It is also useful as an adjunct in the treatment of nearly all infectious diseases, as it helps other vitamins and minerals work better. Horses should obtain B6 in their normal feed if it includes a little maize. The normal feed will contain enough B complex to make administration of B6 safe on its own, but in humans it must always be taken with B complex.

A lack of vitamin B6 causes travel sickness in small animals.

Vitamin B12, cyanocobalimin

This vitamin is incredibly important in all horse concerns. It has already been mentioned in the sections on cobalt and iron, both of which are synthesised into vitamin B12 in the gut. However, what is often referred to as the intrinsic factor in the stomach is needed for these syntheses to take place, and this factor ceases to operate in times of stress, antibiotic use or sickness. B12 *has* to be given by injection to re-activate the intrinsic factor so that cobalt can be absorbed again. Giving B12 orally is a waste of time and money.

Deficiency signs can range from mild lassitude to serious anaemic conditions, usually accompanied by a sub-normal temperature. Newly-born foals which have not been able to stand up since birth are often miraculously restored to life by 10 ml of vitamin B12 intramuscularly. Any animal that is off its feed for no apparent reason can respond to the same treatment. Often these signs follow the administration of antibiotics, and it should be a rule that if they have to be used, B12 should be given at the same time to offset the side effects like loss of appetite. This is often the main side effect when severe drugs are given. For bad cases of anaemia, a course of vitamin B12 would be preferable to the administration of iron tonics with their unfortunate side effects. The dosage should be 10 ml in the muscle or vein, preferably with VAM daily, if necessary. They are water-based vitamins, so an overdose should not occur.

Vitamin B15, pangamic acid (trade name DADA)

This vitamin is now available again in Australia from your vet. It is invaluable for restoring liver function and is worth using in any case of general debility or sickness. The Russians pioneered it in humans, and found its main use was for liver damage and gangrene. It is also a useful tool in cases of copper toxicity, whether caused by mineral or plant, which of course affect the liver. It would be worth using in heliotrope poisoning, for example. Hungerford was also a great believer in this vitamin and every American vet that I know uses it.

Biotin

This is another B vitamin that has suddenly become prominent. Biotin helps hoof growth. Except for seaweed meal, it does not occur naturally in any quantity in normal concentrates unless they consist of whole maize or beans. As always, any form of milling will remove it from grains. It is necessary for hoof and hair growth. Feeding seaweed meal freely to horses has often brought about a remarkably quick response. It definitely works quicker in its natural form than when administered as artificial biotin.

Vitamin C, ascorbate, ascorbic acid, calcium ascorbate, potassium ascorbate, sodium ascorbate

Vitamin C is essential for the health of cells, strength of blood vessels and for collagen synthesis — especially in the pads between the vertebrae and joints. Vitamin C has been used most successfully to cure and alleviate bad backs, particularly in horses when caused by the breakdown of the intervertebral pads (disks). All animals (except humans, some monkeys, some parrots and guinea pigs) manufacture their own vitamin C in the liver from their feed. A horse makes about 30 g+ a day, but under stress of any kind, be it trauma, sickness, travel, poison bites or whatever, the extra demand far exceeds the supply.

In the 1950s, Thomas Hungerford, author of the great book, *Diseases of Livestock*, noted some unexpected results from the use of vitamin C. He remarked that supplementation is always worth trying. The section on vitamin B5 partly explains this, as both vitamin B5 and vitamin C are needed for natural cortisone production.

Vitamin C can be used to control cancer, viral conditions, snake and poison bites, and as an antidote for certain poisons. It is a tremendous help in the treatment of any sickness, as it helps the body, liver and kidneys in particular, to fight back and recover.

Blood vessel fragility in horses, which can be induced by anti-inflammatory drugs, is helped by vitamin C administration. Hesperidin is a part of the C complex, and it would appear to be the factor which helps strengthen blood vessels.

Vitamin C is best given in feed in the form of sodium ascorbate powder, which is tasteless (ascorbic acid powder tastes sour and can also be used in feed, unless the horse is sick, in which case it can be too hard on the gut). However, for practical purposes, I think it is better to use the milder sodium ascorbate. It will not curdle milk and is therefore very useful if handfeeding a foal.

Sodium ascorbate powder (never ascorbic acid) can also be dissolved in distilled water for injection. (A teaspoon of powder makes approximately 5g, but sterile procedures *must* be used.) For intramuscular injection, sodium ascorbate is the preferred variety of vitamin C and must be used for the intravenous route as well.

Injections should be given in the side of the neck following the usual injection procedure — swab the skin, give the horse two sharp slaps and put the needle in on the third, then attach the syringe. The only exception to this is in the case of blackleg (see section in chapter eight). Occasionally, a large injection of vitamin C will leave a slight lump, but it soon goes down.

Vitamin C can be used with complete safety in large amounts for situations where an antibiotic might be used. Many vets use it at the same time as an antibiotic with very satisfactory results. The vitamin has the great advantage that the side effects often associated with antibiotics and antivenene do not occur. When used for snake and other poison bites, it has the advantage of working slightly faster than antivenene, and without the risk of anaphylactic shock. Nor does the variety of snake matter. Vitamin C also has the benefit of being on hand, often as near as the stable fridge. Horses always seem to be bitten by snakes or taken ill at weekends, or when the vet is unobtainable, so vitamin C is a useful standby.

NOTE: *Remember that in cases of shock the veins collapse. Do not waste time looking a vein; use the intramuscular route.*

Many infections now do not respond to antibiotics, and the antibiotics are generally only given to control secondary bacterial infections. Vitamin C, if used in sufficiently large amounts, will cure viral conditions that do not respond to normal drugs, and will cure or prevent the secondary infections as well.

Vaccination and vitamin C

An important fact should be noted. Vaccinations deplete vitamin C in the body to the point of death if the supply is too low. This happened in a case I experienced where a friend's horse travelled for three hours in temperatures of about 42 degrees Celsius. It had been kept on a starved, dry paddock. It was injected with a vaccine for strangles and tetanus in the float before it left. A few hours later (I lived opposite), I noticed it looking very ordinary indeed and went over to ask the owners if they had seen any snakes about, and they said yes. So I raced back home, put 50 ml of sodium ascorbate into a syringe and injected the horse. By that time, it was going down by the back legs, its eyes were nearly closed and it was most distressed. Within minutes of the injection, the horse's eyes opened again and I realised that it was not snakebitten — the pupils were not dilated, as happens in snakebite. It was then that the owner said, 'It must be all right, it's just been vaccinated'. They were lucky that time.

Vitamin E, tocopherol

This is a fat-soluble vitamin which is stored in the body in normal circumstances and acts as an antioxidant. Unlike many other fat-soluble vitamins, it seems to be safe in large amounts. Perhaps the requirement for it is fairly high. Vitamin E is necessary for general good health, and in particular is useful for healing after an injury or trauma. Vitamin E has also been very useful in the aftermath of pneumonia to normalise the breathing rate. It helps to heal the lesions in the lungs; 6–8000 units would be needed daily for a horse under treatment.

It is also helpful, with vitamin A, for fertility problems, especially when allied to a selenium deficiency, as vitamin E is bonded with selenium in some way. As mentioned in the section on selenium, vitamin E can be used to monitor a suspected selenium deficiency. If administering vitamin E produces favourable results rapidly, selenium is lacking and seaweed meal should be put out or the vet consulted for a short-term selenium treatment.

Vitamin E should be found naturally in seeds, unmilled, unboiled and unprocessed grains, wheatgerm and wheat bran, all of which must be fresh. Wheatgerm oil, which should be kept refrigerated, is probably a good source for supplementation if small quantities are needed (*not* soya oil). It is also obtainable in various proprietary forms. I have used White E powder with success. Vitamin E is often supplied with vitamins A and D, both in powdered and injectable form, or is obtainable on its own.

The biggest destroyers of vitamin E are iron, either in tonics, supplements or injections, and liquid paraffin. This should be remembered at all times. It is not often necessary to supplement with iron in Australia. If there is severe anaemia, vitamin B12 injections should be used, as they do not destroy vitamin E. Fish meal (if obtainable) can be a source of extra iron if needed.

Vitamin H, PABA para amino benzoic acid

This vitamin helps the synthesis of folic acid by micro-organisms in the gut. It also offsets the effects of sunburn and sunstroke in humans. Neither condition would normally affect horses unless they were genuine albinos or paint horses with unpigmented skin round the eyes, in which case it would help guard against skin cancer. Horses with these defects should not be bred from in Australia or elsewhere. Skin cancer is painful and it is not a nice way to die. Anyone unfortunate enough to own such a horse could certainly keep it stable by using crushed-up PABA tablets at eight times the human dose. I now find that a great many modern Arab horses have a pink (white streak) down their noses and faces, and I have been told it is a characteristic of the breed in some cases. I cannot believe breeders would countenance a near fatal flaw of this kind. I think the breed groups should do their homework and stop breeding horses that cannot be turned out to grass in a natural state without risk of dying from skin cancer.

Vitamin K, meniodone

This is a fat-soluble vitamin, so it is normally stored in the body. It is needed for normal coagulation of the blood, and is therefore particularly important for all horses. Vitamin K is found in grains, beans, wheatgerm and well-grown organic greenfeed, so it would seem that a deficiency should be rare. However it is very easily destroyed by mineral oil laxatives, oral antibiotics and some drugs. More importantly, it is totally destroyed by irradiation of foodstuffs. This process is becoming more common these days, and there are suggestions that irradiation may be used for grain and some packaged hay (as is sometimes used at shows).

It is best to avoid situations that would destroy the vitamin, but if a deficiency is suspected, and bleeding occurs where the horse's blood fails to clot, it would be a sign to try to stop it and get a vet *quickly*.

Poisons used for small animals that stop blood clotting need vitamin K as an antidote. A vet would be able to advise on quantities and provide the vitamin, which is not currently available over the counter.

6 Non-invasive and natural remedies, and notes on drugs

There are a number of excellent herbal books on the market and Juliette de Bairacli-Levy's *Herbal Handbook for Farm and Stable* is one of the best. One must remember, though, when reading her work, that all of it was done in countries where herbs grew in the pasture naturally and rainfall was, on the whole, regular and plentiful. Chemical fertilisers and sprays were a still a little way down the track. Mary Bromiley has also written an excellent book, *Natural Methods for Equine Health*. When reading this however, again one must remember that fresh herbs are more easily obtained in the United Kingdom.

In Australia, many districts are too dry to grow herbs in any quantity. This has been one of the reasons that I have turned to vitamins and minerals. They *are* always obtainable when animals are off colour. Mrs Grieve's *Modern Herbal* is another book which I find useful. Often, she gives the mineral or other make-up of the herb and one can use it in place of the actual plant. Homeopathy is now being used quite extensively for horses, as are Bach flower remedies and acupuncture. There are good books on all three of these areas — I suggest horse owners study them. Other good sources of information are the works of some of the great early horse vets who used homeopathy quite freely in many cases.

Below are just a few of the natural remedies that I have used successfully with all animals, including equines.

Aloe vera

This is a plant belonging to the cactus family which grows naturally in parts of Australia. Those lucky enough to have the actual plant often use the leaves direct; otherwise it is obtainable in liquid, ointment or gel form. Care should always be taken with any creams and mixtures from plant or other sources that no scents or chemicals have been added; the unadulterated original is the best. Aloe vera can be fed or used externally. On one occasion, I tried the latter on a badly ulcerated wound on a buck goat which I had bought with severe footrot. The feet were easy enough to deal with, but the ulcer, near the hock, was of a longstanding and very obstinate nature. After trying anything and everything without success, aloe vera was able to heal the condition in three days.

Apple cider vinegar

This simple and easily obtainable liquid is invaluable in any country where potassium is in short supply due to chemical farming. Cider vinegar contains natural potassium in a safe form. All fodder stores now carry it in bulk and unpasteurised.

Avoid using the pasteurised variety, as it is not popular with animals, nor is it so effective, having been heated.

Most of the cider vinegar is sold as quadruple strength, so dilute it by four if necessary. It will be too strong to use as a drench otherwise.

Feeding quantities of apples can lead to digestive problems in horses (although chopped apples are reckoned to help with sanding), but they willingly take cider vinegar in large amounts. It is wholly beneficial and a quickly assimilated source of potassium, as well as of other trace minerals. When I first read one of Dr Jarvis's many books on cider vinegar, I did as he instructed and left a container for the horses and goats to help themselves. It may have worked in Maine in the United States, where the deficiencies were not so great, but I could not afford to continue with it freely available in Australia!

Cider vinegar maintains the correct pH in the body, which is probably one of the reasons it is so useful. Because of its potassium content, it is invaluable for mares coming up to foaling. If there is any doubt about potassium levels, start feeding it six weeks before the foal is due. Personally, I feed it all the year round to all stock.

Potassium deficiencies cause blood vessel constriction, affecting the extremities and, it seems, the cervix and uterus in the final stages of pregnancy. Dystokia is the result. I first used cider vinegar on my milking goat herd after a season of very difficult births. The next year I was amazed at the difference; even the largest kids from maiden does arrived relatively easily and in very good health. Many stockowners and human mothers have observed similar effects (I learnt about it too late unfortunately!).

Cider vinegar helps prevent bruising and assists the tissues to recover from exertion. Given regularly to stallions it will help prevent urinary calculi, especially useful if the stallions are limited to very hard bore water — as is the case on many properties in Australia. Cider vinegar added to feed twice a week would be sufficient to stop stones in the urethra or kidneys and prevention is certainly better than cure for this dangerous condition (excessive calcium or a lack of magnesium can also be a contributory factor here). The normal minerals, advocated in the next chapter, must be fed as well. A tablespoon of cider vinegar twice a week would be enough for a stallion.

Cider vinegar can also be used as a mild cure for skin conditions like ringworm when it is too close to the eyes to use a copper wash; rubbing it in well two or three times a day for a couple of days is usually enough. Those wishing to learn more about cider vinegar should read any of Dr Jarvis's very interesting little books on the subject. There are various editions obtainable.

Arnica montana

This is a perennial herb that grows in the mountains of Europe and is now being cultivated successfully in Australia. It is best used in homeopathic tinctures and pillules, and an ointment is available in health shops. In homeopathic form it is an excellent painkiller. I have used it post-operatively with astonishing results. One dog had no idea she'd had an operation, and did not try to scratch or lick the site at all. It also seems to have a healing effect; the same dog healed without a scar from an operation to remove a salivary gland which required about fourteen stitches, as well as two drainage tubes.

Also, as is the case with vitamin C, arnica is good for shock or trauma. In one case, for example, a two-year-old thoroughbred slipped from her handler and galloped straight down the middle of a busy freeway, and went clean over one car into another. The owner insisted we use a drug-free regime (this was in Queensland), and I told him to get a homeopath to provide both oral arnica and a spray for the wounds, which were multiple all over her body. They also used homeopathic calendula, which is marvellous for healing. The result by any standards was impressive. The owner's dedication was incredible. Once we established that the mare had not broken any bones, it was still out of the question to get her to the beach. So he went and collected a few 20-litre containers of seawater and regularly hosed her with it. A week later she was nearly sound, and in two weeks the huge haematoma from her chin to below her brisket was clearing up naturally. She received massive amounts of vitamin C (50 ml at a time) by intravenous injection and oral sodium ascorbate until the healing was well on the way. She also received vitamin E powder, and all the supportive therapy possible.

One month later, she was turned out in some fertile hill country with everything healed up and healthy. Arnica was the only painkiller used, contrary to modern protocol on this subject. She had been a mass of contused and bloody wounds.

An old book on veterinary homeopathy recommends that arnica should be the first mode of treatment in all cases, regardless of the injury or symptoms, as it calms the patient completely. It is available from good herbal and homeopathic doctors, and nowadays some vets. 200 c is the potency most often used for horses, administered either as pillules or drops. Pillules were used on the filly discussed earlier.

Comfrey

The old folk name for comfrey was knit-bone because it helped heal broken bones. It is a broad-leaved plant that grows quite readily in the damper, cooler areas. It will not thrive without plenty of water. Unfortunately comfrey tends to die back in the winter, but can sometimes be kept going in a sheltered frame where it is protected from frosts. Otherwise dry some during the summer and keep it for winter use.

In spite of much publicity to the contrary, the whole plant is completely safe, both internally and externally. In many parts of Germany and also Japan, comfrey is used exclusively for dairy cattle fodder during the summer months; it is highly nutritious and of great assistance used internally or topically for bone problems, including breaks.

Comfrey is one of the few plants that contains natural vitamin B12. This may be one of the reasons why it is so useful in cases of sickness. It may be used in poultices and will often reduce bony swellings like splints of recent origin in a matter of days. It may be made into an ointment or used as a liquid obtained by boiling the leaves; distilled comfrey oil is the best if obtainable. All forms are useful at some time or other. The plant also has the reputation as an inhibitor of cancer.

The best way to feed comfrey is to offer a few leaves to horses once or twice a week; they appear to find it very palatable. In the United Kingdom, most racing stables have a bed of it by the barns and feed each horse a few leaves a week.

Emu oil

This is now readily obtainable from chemists, fodder stores and breeders. It is one of the by-products of emu farming. The oil should be odourless, with no additives. It is quickly absorbed through the skin, and is very helpful in cases of deep-seated joint injury. In horses, it has reduced bony swellings in the same manner as comfrey.

Garlic

This is an onion-like plant that will grow prolifically if kept damp and well fed. Either the bulbs or the chopped leaves may be given. It is also available in oil-filled capsules or tablet form. Garlic, like onions, contains natural sulphur, and sometimes reduces the incidence of interior parasites. There have been one or two suggestions recently that it is crucial to healthy bones as well.

It is a natural antibiotic, and is especially useful in intestinal disturbances. Garlic also has the reputation of being a vermifuge, but although it undoubtedly helps, in my experience it cannot entirely take the place of a balanced diet with the correct amounts of copper. It is now obtainable chopped in bulk ready to add to feed, and is used in the horse racing industry in this way. In cases of sickness in any stock, persuading them to eat garlic in some form can only be beneficial. It can be blended or offered whole; one must experiment.

Hydrogen peroxide (H_2O_2)

This substance is either the oldest antibiotic or the newest, depending on which way you look at it. For cleaning wounds, disinfecting navel cords or any other infection that cannot be resolved, it is invaluable. In the dairy industry, the worst kind of mastitis organisms, such as klebsiella, which will not respond to vitamin C or anything else, are totally gone in three days of intra-mammary H_2O_2 application. I advise the use of six per cent (or a doubled up three per cent) peroxide mixed with 2 ml to 10 ml of pure (not reticulated) water.

As a disinfectant for wounds, it is without equal. It should be applied to the affected area once only and all pathogens will be killed. It has even been used, in the ratios mentioned, to resolve uterine tumours in cows. A fortnight of daily douching with a teaspoon of hydrogen peroxide to a litre of water is required.

It is always safer to use the slightly lower strengths and then there is no chance of a misread dosage being used.

Seaweed products

Seaweed meal is marketed as just that, or as kelp powder with various trade names. The important thing to check is that there are no additives in it, such as urea, and that the minerals in it are as nature intended, not chelated additions (both can occur in seaweed liquids). There are several firms processing seaweed from the southern oceans of Australia and the far northern oceans of the world. Unfortunately, there is pollution in the sea, as the great ecologist Rachel Carson, author of *Silent Spring*, certainly found in 1962. However, seaweed is still the safest and best fodder supplement that we have. In the Appendix I have listed the names of various seaweed products that seem to work well and are as pure as possible.

The section in this book on iodine shows the necessity of using seaweed meal to ensure the continued health of our horses. When I visited trainers at Newmarket in England in 1988, I mentioned that many Australians were rather reluctant to use it. This was regarded with amazement. Apparently every racing stable in England now uses seaweed products. It should always be fed on demand, *not* mixed in with the feed.

The analysis below shows the amazing amount of trace minerals present in seaweed. These are all in organic form and in balance, ensuring that no toxicity can occur.

In earlier books, I advised feeding it carefully according to the type of horse. However, no one seemed to get it right and some most unfortunate symptoms occurred. The mildest effect from feeding too much seaweed is that horses will break out; the worst is that they go somewhere near stark raving mad. 'Breaking out' for those who have not met the term before, is rather like when humans get acne from over-rich feeding; spots come up, usually round the lower neck and wither area.

Average analysis of seaweed meal

Variety: *Ascphyllum nodosum*

Element	%	Element	%
Aluminium	.19300	Osmium	trace
Antimony	.000142	Palladium	trace
Barium	.001276	Platinum	trace
Berylium	trace	Phosphorus	.211000
Bismuth	trace	Lead	.000014
Bromine	trace	Potassium	1.280000
Cadmium	trace	Radium	trace
Calcium	1.904000	Rhodium	trace
Cerium	.019400	Rubidium	.000005
Boron	trace	Selenium	.000043
Caesium	trace	Silicon	.164200
Chromium	trace	Strontium	.074876
Copper	.000635	Sulphur	1.564200
Chlorine	3.680000	Tellurium	trace
Fluorine	0.032650	Thallium	.000293
Gallium	trace	Thorium	trace
Germanium	.000005	Titanium	.000012
Iodine	.062400	Tin	.000006
Indium	trace	Tungsten	.000033
Irridium	trace	Uranium	.000004
Lantanum	.000019	Vanadium	.000531
Magnesium	.213000	Zinc	.003516
Manganese	.123500	Zirconium	trace
Mercury	.000190	Iron	.089560
Molybdenum	.001592	Silver	.000004
Nickel	.003500	Sodium	4.180000
Cobalt	.001227	Niobium	trace
Lithium	.000007	Gold	.000006

Reprinted from *Eco-Ag*, October 1989. Data from Norwegian Seaweed Institute, as reported in *Review of Seaweed Research*. Research series No 76, Clemson University, 1968.

These effects do not occur if horses have seaweed meal available for them to take freely. In the long run it is cheaper that way. Containers on the side of the stable or shelter should be built to contain seaweed in one half and rock salt in the other. The owners may be amazed at how much — or how little — will disappear. Check the section on iodine for the signs of deficiency and excess.

We now find that this is by far the safest way of supplying it. In one example, about one hundred miniature ponies on shocking soil were 'down on their bumpers' (walking on their pasterns), and their joints clicked. It took ten days to get the analysis through and in that time they ate 250 kg of seaweed meal. Both symptoms by this time had disappeared. They have hardly touched the seaweed since, as they know they have had enough!

Drugs — What one should know about them

One of the advantages of using vitamin C is that it has no serious side effects. Any student of medicine will know that all drugs have their disadvantages. The question is whether the good the drug does outweighs its ill effects.

Antibiotics

These drugs have undoubtedly saved many lives in animal and human populations, however, indiscriminate use of different antibiotics is one of the main reasons why they often will not work now. It appears that once organisms are resistant to a drug, this effect can last into the next generation. This result has been observed in experimental rats in laboratory conditions. For those wishing to read more on this subject, consult the book *The Plague* by Charles Gregg, and the article by

Sharon Begley with the title, 'The End of Antibiotics', which is mentioned in the Bibliography.

If an antibiotic has to be used, a sensitivity test should be done to ascertain if it will be effective (this was taught to me by the clinical centre of the University of Melbourne). It was in a sub-clinical mastitis outbreak that I learnt about the short life of antibiotics. If they *must* be used, always make sure that an injection of vitamin B12 (10 ml) is given at the same time. This will help offset the major side effect. Antibiotics affect the villi in the intestines, making them shrivel up and causing an aching gut in the process.

On one occasion, I was advised to shoot about half my herd, as they had mastitis and had built up resistance to every available drug. I bought them when they were quite old; they would have been able to have one drug only used on them, as they had been given all the others. The younger ones could be given penicillin or any other drug of choice as they had never had antibiotics before. This work was done by the University of Melbourne.

I declined to treat or destroy any of them and found safer, more effective methods of cure and prevention by using dolomite as a carrier for the necessary calcium and magnesium. (In countries with very rich soil like the United Kingdom, the United States and New Zealand it is necessary to add a little copper sulphate as well.) I learned that by improving the health of the animals and making sure that they received the necessary dolomite in their feed, mastitis and other similar diseases could not and did not become a factor. However, I was constantly hoping that a safe alternative would be found to antibiotics, and eventually learnt about vitamin C and its curative powers.

Viruses do *not* respond to antibiotics. They are only used to control secondary (usually bacterial) infections which may arise later. Dr Albrecht in the USA (and through him the

Acres USA publication) has frequently pointed this out. In cases of these infections, check the soil and the fodder, and make sure that the calcium to magnesium level is correct. It is often incorrect in many manufactured foods and unhealthy paddocks.

Make sure that a vet prescribes the drug your stock may need and *never* borrow a drug from another farmer or friend (vitamins do not come under this category). Vets tell me that when they give vitamin C with drugs, quite often the good effects are enhanced and the bad ones minimised. Bear in mind the information in chapter five on vitamin B12, and always insist that an injection of this is given with an anti-biotic if one has to be used. A vet demonstrated this to me years ago with a mare that had been very ill with colitis X; the B12 undoubtedly helped her intestinal flora, so she regained her appetite and recovered.

One of the reasons we have virtually run out of antibiotics is the frequency with which they have been used — in many cases where good nutrition and nursing would have been successful. Horses or other animals are given powerful drugs because the owners do not feel like doing the work involved in more natural methods. We have taken the easy option, little realising that new drugs cannot be found indefinitely. One cannot blame the veterinary profession for this — owners always want a quick fix to any problem.

Butazolidin (Btz, Bute)

This is an anti-inflammatory drug that is quite often used on performance horses. However, as residues of this drug or its derivatives have been found in export beef in the United States, there is a possibility that it may be banned and some clinics are advising that these substances should not be used any more. Anti-inflammatories are painkillers, they are sometimes used in arthritic conditions and there may be a belief that they are growth promotants as well, which is perhaps how they were found in beef. In 2003, BTZ is still being used, however.

The use of painkillers has to be thought through. Obviously if pain stops a horse eating, a little arnica or similar must be used, but if it is a leg injury, the painkiller may make the horse use the limb too much. A vet demonstrated this to me many years ago.

Now that arnica is coming into widespread use, there is a safe substitute for other kinds of painkillers, and the case of the terribly damaged racehorse mentioned in the arnica section earlier is a mild illustration.

Remember that butazolidin and many other anti-inflammatories have one rather dangerous side effect — they weaken blood vessels, often to the point where internal haemorrhaging will cause death. The best course of action is to cure the cause of the pain, not mask it with butazolidin or anything else. If it still *has* to be given, make absolutely sure that some vitamin C is given at the same time. This strengthens blood vessels, and so may avert a disaster. It does look as though this particular drug is on the way out, however, now that we have a safe substitute.

Cortisone

In the section on vitamin B5, I explained the mechanism for making cortisone naturally in the body. In humans, giving cortisone in its artificial form inhibits the output of natural cortisone for up to two years and has a reputation for causing cancer. I do not think anyone has found out what it does to horses, but I imagine it would be similar. So in any condition where cortisone would be indicated, such as infections, give extra vitamin C. If the horse has been fed barley, the vitamin B5 levels should be in good order. A lack of magnesium means low levels of all B vitamins.

Hormones

Any form of hormones or steroids is best avoided if possible, as the after-effects can be rather traumatic. My first experience put me off. A fox terrier bitch belonging to my parents was covered by the wrong dog. The vet (in the United Kingdom) said there would be no problem, he would give her a hormone injection (stilboestrol in that instance) to make her abort. The bitch was dead from cancer of the uterus within five months. I know that drugs and methods of administration have improved over the years, but I still have not seen or heard anything that makes me think that one does not pay for the use of such substances. The body is not geared to manage the often unknown side effects. If steroids have been used, remember that they have the effect of stopping the absorption of calcium and magnesium. They also either stop the synthesis of vitamin A or render it unobtainable, so the intake of those minerals and vitamins would possibly have to be increased.

I discovered that large animals given hormones for ovum transplant programs seemed to have persistent vitamin A deficiency troubles for the next two years. Often the deficiency was so great after hormone administration that they could not hold to service or breed normally for that period without considerable amounts of extra cod-liver oil (vitamin A and D). Shortage of that vitamin (and low copper levels) is the biggest cause of poor breeding performance. Any animal that has dried off with stilboestrol shows the same symptoms. It can take a whole lactation before milk production returns to normal. After all, stilboestrol is a male hormone which would be contra-indicated in a lactating animal. Drying off a mare with stilboestrol is not recommended because it acts too quickly and often causes mastitis. The old-fashioned method of making vinegar poultices is still an effective way of drying up a milking animal if there is a good reason for doing so. A bitch whose puppies had been killed at five days was dry in thirty-six hours using this method. It would not take much longer with a mare (if an orphan could not be found to replace the lost foal or whatever).

However, in some breeding programs, hormones have to be used, especially for artificial insemination when using a stallion in another country. Ovum transplants could not be performed if we did not have hormones; in these cases, regular supplementation with cod-liver oil must be an ongoing part of the program — which should include the normal minerals in the feed as well. If this is not done, there will be abortions and the whole process will be wasted.

Anthelmintics (interior parasite preventatives)

Thanks to the work of Dr W A Albrecht, we know that interior parasites are caused by unhealthy land for two reasons. One is that dung beetles will not be working to process the manure and the other is that horses do not receive adequate copper from poor land. Nowadays, our soils are nowhere near what they should be, and possibly will not be so in the foreseeable future, so copper sulphate and sulphur (with dolomite) are added to the feed, and seaweed is made freely available. When I worked in racing in England in the 1950s, worming horses just didn't figure. All animals were viewed as having a few worms, and some horses in racing used to pass two metre samples, yet these horses were fit and winning races. I feel that it is not the worms that are the culprit, but the lack of top-class, healthy feed.

All anthelmintics contain a poison, or they would not work.

Because they are not made (these days) from natural substances, resistance to them has to become a fact of life. I was doing a talk for the local Department of Agriculture a few years ago, and the convenor said as he introduced me, 'I hope you have some answers to worms, because the drenches are becoming redundant faster than replacements can be made.'

Fortunately I do, and it is basically called good management. Organic certification cannot include the use of these substances, or chemicals that destroy exterior parasites, and both are equally easy to prevent. Those who have read the section on sulphur will realise the great uses of that natural substance.

One of the facts that spelled out the demise of several drenches was their toxic after-effects. Manure was not processed in the normal fashion by worms and dung beetles, and some other brands caused the deaths of chickens who scratched round the horse yards. In recent times, some drenches have actually caused the death of the recipients; in one case the vet rather apologetically told the owner that it happened occasionally! It would be interesting to know whether these animals die from anaphylaxis or if the drench is cumulative or just unstable in its effects. Large doses of vitamin C prevented death in two other cases where the owners rang me in time.

Exterior parasite preventatives

Exterior parasites only attack animals whose sulphur levels are inadequate, or animals that have sugar (from molasses) in their blood. Unfortunately much of our land is sulphur deficient — I had hardly ever seen lousy animals until I came to

Australia in 1959, but when visiting the United Kingdom in 1996 I found that nearly all dairy cows had lice! Sulphur is inhibited by artificial fertilisers. These were not in general use when I left the United Kingdom, but now ammonium nitrate and superphosphate are used regularly. Check the section on sulphur and it will be seen how incredibly important it is for full health.

Horses do not often get lice, because they are usually fed fairly well, but in some parts of Australia ticks are a problem. Large numbers are only found on sour, poor land. Land that has been properly remineralised and is on the climb back to good health is not a haven for ticks.

Vaccinations

See section in chapter eight and the section on vitamin C in chapter five.

7 Basic feeding practice

This chapter explains how to incorporate the necessary minerals in the feed safely and easily. Those used to buying a bag of pellets or something similar may find this quite difficult at first. A little perseverance is needed — I have been feeding all stock this way for about thirty-five years and it has become second nature!

The necessity for mineral supplements

In one well-researched review on horse nutrition relating especially to racehorses, it states that if the ingredients of the ration are of high quality and grown on ground containing the required nutrients, no supplementation of minerals or vitamins should be necessary. This is quite true, but no longer feasible.

Sadly, nowadays there are few if any places in the world that can lay claim to a perfectly balanced soil, least of all Australia. Even the famous horse pastures of the world like Kentucky and Ireland are being treated with artificial fertilisers, and a steep rise in copper deficiencies has been the result. The analysis in chapter two will be somewhere nearer the mark. So to keep our horses healthy, whatever their job, supplementation will be necessary.

Sixty years ago in Southern England, Argentinian oats (because they were harder than English oats), fresh-cut oaten chaff (for some horse disciplines it was cut on the premises the same day) and best quality bran were the basic parts of the feed ration in racing stables. Grass and clover hay were carefully selected, and was preferably a year old and from parts of the country known to have good soil. Occasionally a few sunflower seeds were added to the ration, but lucerne chaff and lucerne hay did not figure, probably due to the fact that there was always plenty of greenstuff available in the United Kingdom. In one racing stable, raw sugar was used experimentally for a season just after World War Two and produced very gratifying results (it was easier to put through the feed than molasses). However we now know that neither is a good long-term option, as they interfere with calcium/magnesium synthesis and encourage biting insects. Honey is as nature made it and (though rather sticky) is safe to use. A printout received from the *Milton Times* confirmed that horses had died when their feed was contaminated with pellets fed to cattle.

The only form of mineral supplementation in the leading jumping stable (with about twenty-five per cent of useful gallopers as well) where I worked was to give them a sod of earth, grass and all. This was about thirty centimetres cubed in size and was cut out of a very good paddock that we kept especially for the purpose. It was given with the evening feed and next morning it had generally completely disappeared. This could be done in those days because the soil, even in the United Kingdom, was still in good heart — that regime would not be effective there today either.

Grains

Our grains, be they oats, barley, maize or linseed, are now almost invariably grown on depleted soils which have been artificially fertilised. Therefore they will be lacking in calcium and/or magnesium and or sulphur, as well as trace minerals like copper, cobalt, boron and selenium. All of these are incredibly important. It must be remembered that as soon as grains are milled or heated the vitamins in them are lost, which is most undesirable.

Some people prefer to feed oats and some barley — the former can be fed straight or bruised, the latter soaked — so the dissolvable minerals can be incorporated in the feed, and the cider vinegar can be included in the water used for soaking the grain. If possible, barley should make at least half the grain ration and more would not hurt. Many years ago when I first read Juliette de Bairacli Levy's book, *Herbal Handbook for Farm and Stable*, I took her advice and chose barley as the main grain in all rations. It worked very well with horses and milking animals, keeping the butterfats in the latter at a constant and causing no heating up problems in horses, so I have stuck with it.

Vitamin B5 (pantothenic acid) and barley

Information about vitamin B5 in chapter five was not generally known in those days, and it partly explains why barley is so valuable as a component of feed. Barley is possibly the best source of vitamin B5. It is needed by horses and all animals to synthesise their own cortisone. As long as B5 and vitamin C are present, this synthesis takes place automatically. (A horse makes more than 30 g of vitamin C in its liver daily.) In Russia in the 1950s (and possibly still today), racehorses were fed barley grain and barley hay almost exclusively and appeared to perform very well on it. Barley is not quite as heating as oats and is therefore often the preferred grain for horses in medium work.

Bran

This is made from wheat and bears absolutely no resemblance to what we called broad bran in the old days — modern bran would have been returned to the supplier as pollards! Bran is necessary to act as a mild laxative and to provide the sulphur (a component of wheat if it is grown on a paddock where the sulphur was adequate). Bran provides the bulk that keeps the horse's system working. It is also useful for bran mashes which, made with boiled linseed, are easy to digest and soothing to the insides of a tired horse. When organically grown, wheat is the main source of natural sulphur and it is from this grain that bran is milled. But according to the CSIRO, conventional farming methods have totally eliminated sulphur from the feed chain. This is unfortunate, as sulphur is needed to help assimilate selenium and to ensure horses do not get external parasites.

Bulk

Horses need a bulky ration, even for racing. Protein cannot be fed to the exclusion of carbohydrates; the two should be kept in balance. A ration too high in protein merely leads to digestive and metabolic troubles. This is especially so if the

source of the protein is legumes (see below). Very rapid depletion of iodine will follow with its attendant disadvantages.

Other options

Maize which supplies vitamin B6 in your horse's feed, but not
more than about ten per cent.

A tablespoon of **sunflower seeds** a day — (they are too
oily and can cause skin problems when given in excess).

Copra (coconut meal) can also be included. This is a balanced meal mineralwise and should be chemical-free.

The original samples I saw in the late 1980s were too high
in organophosphates and the analysis I was sent was about
eight per cent contaminated with them. I consulted a
NASAA (National Association for Sustainable Agriculture
Australia) inspector and he told me that transporting the feed
in contaminated trucks could do the damage. I took it up with
the producers and they now transport copra in contamina-
tion-proof bags. It is a balanced feed additive, and often useful
to add to older horses' rations if their teeth are not too good.

Not more than a tablespoon per day of **rice pollards** should
be used.

Linseed also can be added for making bran mashes
(linseed must be be boiled for at least four hours). These are
about the only additives I would suggest.

Animals do not need changes in their feed like humans
seem to, and once settled into a feed regime they do very well
on a steady diet!

Basic ration

The basic ration should comprise equal parts lucerne and
oaten chaff, both of which should be as freshly milled as possible, and bran (all by bulk, not weight). To this, half of one

of the above parts of grain should be added (this will be one sixth of the ration).

The feed should not exceed a two litre measure when all mixed together. For a horse in light work, half of the above will be enough. It should be fed once or twice a day, depending on the work the horse is doing (and the time available to the owner!).

Dampening feed

This was not necessary in the past, as dusty feeds were unknown prior to the advent of artificial fertilisers in the 1950s. Horse rations were not dampened at all; dusty feed was sent smartly back to the supplier. Nowadays all feed is dusty, the price we pay for chemical farming, and it is very necessary to damp it down to prevent the horses inhaling the dust as they feed; this has caused permanent lung damage in the past.

Adding the minerals (for a full grown horse)

Dolomite and sulphur do not dissolve and thus are mixed with the bulk of the dry feed (the two chaffs and bran) as follows:
> One tablespoon of dolomite per *feed*;
> One tablespoon of milling sulphur (as sold for orchard use) per *day* (split between the two feeds); and
> Copper and other trace minerals if needed (according to shortfalls in the paddock analysis).
> (Also see the Appendix.)

The trace minerals, copper sulphate, cobalt sulphate and boron, can all be dissolved. As a rule, only copper is needed; I recommend a *minimum* of 5 g (a teaspoon) per day per horse. If the land analysis shows up poor cobalt or boron shortfalls, about 2 g a week of cobalt sulphate and boron can be added depending on the requirement (see the ailments chapter).

Administration

The easy way to do this is to dissolve the copper sulphate (and whatever else) in a little hot water, then add the required cider vinegar of about 3 ml per day (the vinegar is usually quadruple strength). If the horses are not getting grain, this mixture can have a little water added and can be used for dampening the feed (very lightly). This mix can be made up once a week after a little arithmetic. One seventh of it should be put on the feed each day.

> NOTE: This cannot ferment or go bad; vinegar is a very old-fashioned and efficient preservative, and copper sulphate stops pathogens forming.

Feeding extra grain

When barley or other grain is fed, the copper, vinegar and water can be added to the water in which the grain is soaked. Barley absorbs half its bulk in water in twenty-four hours (an eight litre bucket of barley absorbs four litres of liquid).

Water

Rain water or bore water must be used where possible, as many of the additives in reticulated water can have adverse effects on the horse's system. Sodium fluoride salts inhibit magnesium, without which the gut and muscle enzymes cannot function at all, as well as depleting vitamins A and D.

Chlorine is not very desirable either, but in a trough situation it usually volatilises and goes. But the smell in water straight out of the pipe can put off animals (and people).

Actual amounts

The amounts given above in the bulk of this section are often more than enough for a horse in light work. When all the minerals are present in the feed the requirement is much smaller, and the horse makes full use of what it is given. Horses in strong work can have more as they need it.

A kilogram measure of feed once a day is enough for most horses, as long as they have good grazing and pasture hay as well (both from remineralised paddocks).

Quarter horses and Arabs

Quarter horses and Arabs are generally very good 'doers'. They do not need as much feed as, say, a thoroughbred. They can have two feeds a day if the work or condition of the animal warrants it, but it will be unlikely; they are both very tough horses. A quarter horse I acquired in a very degraded condition needed two feeds a day for about a week, and then once a day with good grazing and hay; once he was right and his feet had grown out again, anything more than two hard feeds a week was too much — they are very tough animals.

Performance horses

Hunters in the United Kingdom (expected to hunt eight hours a day, three days a fortnight) had six feeds a day, and racehorses three or four. The trainer/owner of the horse will soon know if the feed is too high or not high enough.

Made-up and/or extruded (pelletised) feeds

Many firms produce made-up feeds. These come in ready-mixed form and some are better than others. The disadvantages are that it is a more expensive way of feeding and the quality of the original ingredients is not known. To be extruded or pelletised, the feed is heated as well. Generally, the feeds are mixed with molasses and quite significant amounts of salt are frequently added, all to increase palatability. There have been cases of horses developing oedema due to the high salt content of some ready-mixed feeds.

The greatest disadvantage is that the horse owner cannot know the quality of the materials used to make up the feed, whereas when the materials are bought in their basic form, one can see immediately if any of it is not top quality.

It is always more satisfactory to make up one's own feeds. Read the section on botulism in chapter eight for the reasons.

Molasses

Molasses and all forms of sugar must be avoided in any feeds. Work done in the United States and the United Kingdom in recent years suggests that flies like to bite horses with sugar in their veins. We know of three illnesses carried by blood transfer (and there may be more): anthrax, EIA (Equine Infectious Anaemia or horse AIDS) and Ross River virus. It is not worth taking a chance with any of them. Sulphur (check the section in chapter four) in the feed will also help to discourage biting flies and mosquitoes. One has to remember that the racehorse in the next stall or hack in the next stable at an event or show may be carrying Ross River virus or EIA.

Molasses also interferes with the synthesis of calcium and magnesium in horses, just as sugar does in humans.

> NOTE: Ross River virus is almost invariably referred to as Ross River fever.

Vitamin C

Sodium ascorbate (non-acidic vitamin C) powder can be

added to feeds for horses who are under the stress of very hard work and travel. A tablespoon a day for three days before the journey makes everything work much better, and incidents like the one in the section on magnesium in chapter four should not occur.

Feeding legumes

As mentioned in the section on iodine, iodine deficiency problems are minimal in Europe because most of the soils contain it naturally. Also, these days seaweed meal is frequently fed there. Lucerne hay and chaff are not generally used, as they are goitragenic feeds (which deplete iodine; see section on iodine in chapter four). But in Australia and the United States, lucerne chaff is always used and frequently lucerne hay as well, to say nothing of other legumes. When this kind of feeding is practised, extra iodine supplementation must be given if horses are to realise their potential, or indeed stay healthy at all, as Australia is almost entirely iodine deficient. The most effective way to do this is to have seaweed meal freely available for all horses all the time.

All legumes deplete iodine, and some do it faster than others. Soya is the worst in this respect and tends to store aluminium as well.

Seaweed meal

This is an excellent source of natural iodine and should be freely accessible to all horses (and kept dry in paddock situations). The amount they take may cause some astonishment at first, but they (or any other animal) do not take more than they need. They leave it strictly alone when they don't require it and they know better than we do! Horses on Newmarket Heath in the United Kingdom on 1988, apparently all supplemented with seaweed products, looked as good as I remembered them, not overweight and in good, hard condition. The one I rode was in very good form!

Hay

All horses need the best quality hay available and great care must be taken to see that it is not mouldy. In stables it is usually fed in a hay net or hay racks. The latter are less work and are now coming back into fashion, as they are easier to fill than hay nets.

Good grass or mixed pasture hay, especially from remineralised pastures, is *excellent* feed. Lucerne hay, often grown on irrigation land with phosphatic fertilisers, is totally undesirable. First-cut, dry-land lucerne in *small* quantities can be fed *with* the pasture hay. The more species of good grasses and legumes in a paddock, the better (the old gurus looked for and got between forty-five and sixty-five varieties of mixed grasses, legumes and beneficial herbs). Another factor that has to be remembered is that the ambient temperature can make a big difference to the food requirements of horses in strong work. For example, English racehorses or hunters (the latter had to be very fit indeed, and maintain it for a six-month season) need about 10 $1/2$ kg of oats or similar a day. In warmer countries, horses in the same kind of work would do quite well on 6–7 kg or possibly less. The extra was required in Europe to keep the animals' temperatures up in the colder weather — in other words, energy is used keeping warm.

(Also see the Appendix.)

Feed fashions

Some years ago there was a vogue for feeding mostly pollards and chopped carrots to show horses. The results were tragic.

One kept hearing that this or that horse had died, either of colic or its follow-on in many cases, twisted gut. There was not enough bulk in the feed to keep the horses' insides in order.

Another feed, also in popular use some years ago, was cottonseed meal. Unfortunately, most horse owners found out too late that it caused chronic kidney trouble, and in most cases seemed to be incurable. Apparently it can also cause male infertility, also an undesirable consequence. The reason for the damage caused by this meal is a constituent called gossipel, which has to be heated to dispel the poison factor or it is liable to cause the trauma mentioned. In about 1980, it was discovered that once the cottonseed was cooked, its nutritive value was fully available to the horse with no ill effects. When properly processed it may be an excellent feed, but when buying feeds containing cottonseed meal, check that it has been cooked, and have it tested for sprays. Cotton has the unenviable reputation of being one of the most heavily sprayed crops in the world.

Requirements

Horses need food that they have to digest, in other words bulk, no matter what their job is in life. The amount of protein in the feed should be adjusted according to the horse's work program. The oaten, lucerne chaffs and bran combination mentioned earlier comes out as about twelve to thirteen per cent protein. Even the highest protein feeds must be balanced by the same amount or more of carbohydrates, otherwise the horse's digestion will break down.

Good hay, of course, can supply bulk. Many people do not realise that even the chaffs and bran contain protein. The general impression is that first class protein is the only one that matters. A diet of that alone would kill. An interesting book on the heavy horses of London in the 1800s showed that they were fed almost solely on beans, oaten chaff and grass hay — a balanced diet — and their workload — twelve hours at a stretch — was mind-boggling.

Vitamins A and D

This occurs in its natural state as cod-liver oil and 5 ml a week is usually enough. As with seaweed meal, horses know when they need it, and will soon make their preferences felt. Cod-liver oil must be purchased in a lightproof container, as vitamins are killed by light.

Linseed grain

A cupful of linseed grain should be added to four litres of water, then boiled for at least four hours before being fed in small quantities. It makes a good addition to any feed. A cup or two of the liquid can be added to the rations of several horses or it can be used to make a bran mash to finish off a day of extra hard work.

Number of feeds per day

The number of feeds per day depends on the time and man-power at one's disposal. Hunters used to be fed six times a day, starting at 6 a.m. and ending at 10 p.m., but they had to be capable of hunting eight hours a day, three days a fortnight. Now, they probably get two or three feeds a day like all other horses. Horses at grass seem to do well on one afternoon feed daily, but if the pasture is poor they will need feeding twice daily with their minerals added and hay as well.

Horses on a completely remineralised and balanced pad-dock will want very few extras. Seaweed and one small feed daily should be plenty, but this *must* include their copper ration as well as the dolomite and sulphur.

Amounts of feed

Since writing the first edition of this book ten years ago, I have discovered, to my horror, that many horse owners have no idea on this subject at all. I would say 2 litres (by bulk) in one or two feeds a day is the maximum required for a horse in ordinary work (exercising for about fifteen kilometres a day).

A litre measure a day for the lightly-ridden pleasure hack is plenty, sometimes too much! I do not expect to have to tell trainers and owners of high performance horses how much to feed, as one rides them in their work, the need for less or more is quite apparent.

Rehabilitation

In the past few years, my horse has always been a semi-retiree, and usually very run down, on loan or given to me because it was considered to be geriatric (like me!). In this case, a one kg measure of feed made up as above, twice a day initially, plus a biscuit of hay if the paddock feed was not enough, usually has to be cut rather hastily to one feed or less a day.

Once the minerals are available, horses make far more use of their feed.

In one case, a horse which had competed in world class events went back to full-time showjumping as a school horse at eighteen years of age, as a result of this regimen. The old quarter horse came in an awful state, but went back to full-time campdraughting (he came to me incredibly poor at twenty-three), and was winning and also working as a school horse. Once the minerals and feed are balanced, very little feed is needed to maintain a horse in top condition unless it is doing very hard work. But a great many people have horses for pleasure and there is no pleasure in a horse that is overfed and possibly underworked!

NOTE: Make sure that dolomite is the actual rock mined out of the ground; there have been enterprising fodder merchants who have made it up with ground limestone and Epsom salts, which is both dangerous and ineffective. By law, all minerals have to be marked on the bag these days. This is not always observed.

I have extended and simplified this chapter, as I am frequently told that it is too complicated. A little time taken reading the whys and wherefores and working out the amounts will soon make it simple!

8 Ailments

There is one question that any horse (or other stock) owner must always ask in any case of illness or sick land — *why*? There is always an answer.

This chapter contains a list of conditions and the reasons for their presence. They are nearly always due to deficiencies, breeding malpractice or unbalanced feeding.

This should help horse keepers pinpoint the likely cause of the trouble. Refer to the appropriate section below, as well as the sections on the minerals or vitamins involved, and remember, *all* the minerals and vitamins listed in the feed chapters are needed.

The list below is for troubleshooting and should help show where an imbalance might be. Often an imbalance can be caused by overfeeding of high protein feed without the work to balance it and this prevents minerals from doing their job.

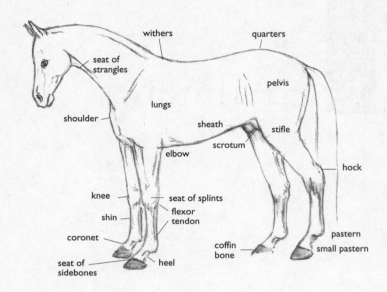

Seats of ailments

Recent work on copper, by Robert Pickering especially, has shown that the higher the protein, the more copper is needed. In most cases, the high protein is not justified anyway.

Conditions due to lack of boron

Arthritis   Soft bones or any malformation

Conditions that can be due to a lack of calcium and/or magnesium

Arthritis   Ringbone
Epiphysitis (open knees)   Prolapse

Deformities
Founder
Kidney or other stones
Mastitis/tetanies
Nervous behaviour
Respiratory ailments

Shin soreness
Strangles
Tetanies
Splints
Stringhalt
Warts

Conditions that can be due to a lack of copper

All fungal diseases
Anaemia
Cancer
Crohn's disease
  (Johne's disease)
Diarrhoea
EPM (protozoa)
Failure to come in season
Fence and bark chewing
Herpes infections
Impaired immune system

Proud flesh
Queensland
  (or Canadian) itch
Rain scald
Ringworm
Seedy toe
White line disease
  (onychomycosis — old
  name, canker)
Windsucking
Worms, coccidia and
  enzootic infections

Conditions due to a lack of vitamin A and D

Abortion
Metritis
Failure to conceive
Infertility in stallions
Kidney stones

Knuckle-over (contracted
  tendons)
Pinkeye (sandy blight,
  conjunctivitis)

Conditions due to a lack of sulphur

Lice or any exterior lodgers
Lack of amino acids in gut (specifically cysteine and methionine)
Inability to assimilate selenium

Conditions due to a lack of potassium

Blood vessel constriction
Dystokia
Navicular disease
Urinary calculi — stones (with magnesium and calcium)

There is a range of conditions, caused by a general lack of minerals and vitamins, as well as those mentioned. These are a few:

Avitaminosis
Brucellosis (Bang's disease)
Colitis X
Crohn's disease
EPM (equine protozoal myeloencephalitis)
Leucopoenia (lack of leucocytes in the peripheral blood)
Tuberculosis

Hereditary conditions covered in this section

HYPP — Hyperkalemic Partial Paralysis
SCID — Severe Combined Immune Deficiency
Those diseases that are plain hereditary would not be a problem if breeders tested foals prone to them at birth and then

made sure they either could not breed or were not allowed to live. This is particularly serious due to the dangerous nature of HYPP, for example, where riders' lives are at risk.

Definition of an ailment

A great many conditions regarded as ailments are often the result of mineral and vitamin imbalances or deficiencies, or the ill-advised use of certain drugs. Even the so-called infectious diseases can be warded off or largely minimised if the horse's mineral (and therefore vitamin) status is correct.

There seems to be a tendency in recent years to give fancy and rather unknown names to many conditions that hitherto had easily-understood ordinary names! Onychomycosis is one of these, and is actually similar to what was called canker in the past. It, like many other conditions, is brought about by the almost total suppression of copper in the food chain due to the continued use of high analysis fertilisers (phosphatic and nitrogenous) worldwide.

Conditions that many horse owners have come to regard as inevitable, such as fence chewing, are only the result of the horse looking for minerals lacking in its grazing and hard feed. All are covered in this section, which should be read with the last chapter on basic feeding practice in mind.

Antibiotics

When any antibiotics are given, a vitamin B12 injection should be administered at the same time. All drugs cause pain in the gut by affecting the lining of the intestines and can make the patient uncomfortable enough to be put off its feed. This does not happen if B12 is given at the same time as the drug. It is good practice to give B12 with any drug, as its effect is to make the patient feel better, which is, after all, the object of the treatment.

Disinfecting — wounds and navel cords

Another fact now emerging is that many people (sometimes, I regret to say, even vets) do not seem to know how to disinfect a wound and set it on the path of healing. Those who do know how these things are done will have to bear with me emphasising this aspect again and again. The amazing recovery of the thoroughbred in chapter six's section on arnica, where all natural methods were used and no sepsis occurred, should be referred to. Against that, is an example of a horse which was disturbed in the stable by a thunderstorm, and cut into its flexor tendon, slightly damaging the sheath and causing a cut of about 8 cm. The vet insisted it be taken to the horse hospital. Five days later they rang to say that the sepsis was so bad the horse would have to be put down. We fought to save it, but we lost.

The vets who taught me many moons ago insisted that all disinfectants inhibited healing, therefore it had to be done only once and *properly*.

Materials generally used are:

Cider vinegar, occasionally

Copper sulphate washes

Hydrogen peroxide (H_2O_2), six per cent solution

Iodine — however, there have been several cases of navel illness where this has been used. It is therefore safer to stick with the two items listed below or alcohol.

Methylated spirits

Surgical spirit

Drenching

It should be noted that drenching does not always mean

worming. Many fluids can be given this way. This does not always mean stomach tubing. A drenching gun that holds 500 ml or more, as used for cattle or sheep, can be quite effective for a horse. Insert the gun into the side of the horse's mouth, point it towards the top of the back of the throat and pump the liquid in slowly. Alternatively, a highly effective method always used in English racing stables in the old days can be used. First, the horse, wearing a head collar with a long rope attached, should be put in a stable with beams or joists overhead. The rope should be thrown over the joist and the head pulled up so that the liquid will pour easily down the throat; this is merely to save the arm of the drencher! The drench to be used is put in a smooth-necked wine bottle, and carefully poured in the side of the horse's mouth. Sometimes the operation is easier (especially if the horse is large) if the drencher stands on the partition between the boxes. A 50 ml syringe will double very well as a drenching gun, and is easier to clean.

> NOTE: *Under no circumstances should liquid paraffin be used (it demineralises the system). A good brand (not soya or canola) of cooking oil can be used instead.*

Painkillers

Most of the information on painkillers was covered in chapter six. Many years ago it was rare to see 'bleeders' (racehorses bleeding from the nostrils after a race). Unfortunately, now it is unusual to go to a race meeting and not see several horses having their noses hastily wiped clean of blood by their attendants as they are being unsaddled. Enquiries into two cases of horses that died of sudden haemorrhages showed that in each case the horse had been on a sustained course of butazolidin. The vet, if consulted, would have suggested giving the horse additional vitamin C in its diet, as this vitamin strengthens the blood vessels. Hesperidin, which is part of the vitamin C complex, is regularly given to bleeders to help cure them in the United Kingdom. Arnica is just as effective and safer if a painkiller is needed.

Ailments

Anaesthetics

Horses are often quite ill after anaesthetics, and there have been several cases where they have failed to recover. If a general anaesthetic should be necessary, give the patient (in its feed) a tablespoon of vitamin C powder daily for four days before the operation and four days after. Better still, have the vet give 15 g (30 ml) intravenously as well, just before administering the anaesthetic. It has been found in tests done on anaesthetising animals that this stops the usual struggling and trauma when the anaesthesia is wearing off. They wake up quite calmly an hour or so after the operation.

The struggles as the patient thrashes about (that many have come to accept as normal) are often the cause of broken legs and damage in horses. No matter how much trouble is taken to make the bed soft, horses are particularly prone to post-anaesthesia injuries. The vitamin C in no way lessens the effect of the anaesthetic, it merely helps the horses throw it off afterwards, and stops any lingering side effects. Several vets have tried this treatment and were very impressed with the results. For local anaesthetics, giving oral vitamin C will help reduce swelling at the site (usually for gelding) and promote healing.

Anthrax, Loodiana fever, horse plague, charbon

This disease was and possibly still is endemic to parts of the Indian continent. In Australia, there are seasonal outbreaks. Some have occurred recently in the irrigation country when the weather is extremely hot and humid. The spores thrive on sour soils in those conditions.

It is best to avoid horse activities in districts where the disease is rampant, as happened in Victoria in 1997. There is some record of it being cured with vitamin C, but the evidence is circumstantial. It would certainly be worth trying, as there do not seem to be any other answers. The vaccine does not work for horses, and does in fact give them the disease immediately — do not try it.

Arthritis

Arthritis is generally due to the incorrect absorption of calcium and magnesium, accompanied by a lack of the mineral boron and possibly copper. These four minerals and vitamins A and D are required for full bone and joint health. The condition of the horse can be much improved if the phosphate-rich grains in the diet are removed and changed to the following:

Equal parts bulk oaten chaff, lucerne chaff and bran
Add to this:
A tablespoon of dolomite per feed
A tablespoon of yellow dusting sulphur a day
Half a teaspoon of borax (sodium borate) a day for nine days, and in very severe cases, one teaspoon for the same amount of time.

Make up enough liquid to dampen the feed. It is easier to make a week's supply at a time, so that each day, the horse gets a cupful of unpasteurised cider vinegar (break it down four to one) and one teaspoonful of copper sulphate. Add rainwater to the mixture. Give 5 ml of cod-liver oil a day, or put 10 ml in a syringe and put it in the horse's mouth every other day for the first nine days. Always feed seaweed meal on demand, so that the horse may take as much or little as it needs. Do the same with salt or leave rock salt out for it. It is necessary to have a remineralised paddock for the horse, and/or organically-grown pasture hay, but do not give lucerne hay.

When making up the feeds, do not exceed a litre (kg) measure each time, then add dolomite and sulphur to the feed and dampen with the water that has cider vinegar, copper sulphate and borax in it. When the horse comes back into work, a *small* amount of whole barley may be given soaked in the above mixture (make up a week's supply at a time). The sooner it does light work the better. In fact, arthritis is always improved by quiet exercise.

On one occasion, a twenty-year-old thoroughbred stallion was in such pain and so badly crippled with arthritis that he could neither be ridden, nor serve his mares. He was treated with the above regimen (without the borax). He improved to the point where he could do light dressage again and serve his mares quite successfully. He lived for another five years. At that time it was not known that a lack of boron as well as an imbalance in the feed was the cause of arthritis. The cure took several weeks; with borax it is a matter of days.

More recently, a famous ex-hurdler, Babble Boy, at thirty-one years of age, was totally crippled with arthritis and unable to move from his paddock shed. He was put on the above regimen (with borax) and in nine days could trot to the gate to greet his owners with his feed and once more enjoy life. He was still alive and well two years later.

In another case, a top dressage stallion of about twelve years of age developed arthritis so badly the vets said it should be put down. It took nine days to get him back in action. Interestingly, the rider had thought that the horse was resisting for the last four years. It was now performing better than it had for that space of time. If you have a horse that is unwilling to do his work for no apparent reason, always suspect arthritis as a base cause and treat it as above if necessary.

Borax is quite safe to use. It was removed from the poisons list in 2001.

Arthritis, (septic) joint ill, navel ill, polyarthritis

Arthritis can sometimes be of septic (infectious) origin. Blood tests will determine this. It can be contracted venereally, from a wound or more usually from the navel cord (in foals). This kind is very difficult to cure, being usually caused by corynebacteria. Massive ongoing doses of vitamin C, at least 20 cc twice daily into the vein for an adult and 15 cc for a foal (also twice daily) might effect a cure. It must be pointed out that often with septic arthritis in foals, the damage is done by the organism before it becomes apparent. This often makes treatment a waste of time, as the joints are frequently found to be permanently damaged.

> NOTE (see below): Use methylated spirits; hydrogen peroxide (six per cent), a teaspoon to half a litre; or a copper sulphate wash for disinfecting the navel cord.

Work done on my animals in the 1960s by the University of Melbourne, and Dr V Sloss in particular, taught me much about this complaint.

A vet and I decided to see if the corynebacter could be

stopped in one particular case. The foal was already damaged, but we decided to have a go. 100 g (200 ml) was given intravenously each day, as well as sodium ascorbate orally. Four to five days later the bacteria was no longer evident. So this treatment *is* sometimes worth trying.

We also had success with a foal who developed septic arthritis at six weeks from a latent navel cord infection. The owner had disinfected with iodine, but it had not worked (the second time this has happened). I told him to keep the vitamin C coming as above, but for longer and the foal recovered, which was quite a victory.

Artificial colostrum

If the mare's own colostrum is unavailable for any reason, an acceptable substitute can be made as follows. To the required quantity of (clean) unpasteurised milk (from a cow or CAE-free goats), add one dessertspoon of cod-liver oil, and one of liquid seaweed (Vitec is suitable, as there are no chelated extras in it). The former will supply the necessary vitamins A and D as well as the oil which will start the gut working to pass the meconium. The seaweed will provide a large range of necessary trace minerals and help boost the orphan's immune system. This formula has been successful with a number of orphans of all kinds.

Colostrum from another mare (who must be disease free) will provide the mechanical properties of the colostrum. However, the immunity comes from a mare to its own foal according to the mare's medical history, rather like a natural vaccine.

Avitaminosis

This occurs in horses whose mineral requirements are nowhere near being met. The condition clears up quite quickly once dolomite, sulphur and copper are added to the diet on a daily basis and seaweed meal made freely available. Initially give 10 ml of VAM (vitamins, amino acids and minerals in liquid form) in the same syringe as 10 ml of vitamin B12 and the same of vitamin C. This will help kickstart the horse's system back into action.

Azoturia

In the past, this unpleasant condition was very common in hunters in the United Kingdom. It happened when there was a freeze up and hunting stopped. Horses that were being fed large quantities of grain suddenly could not be exercised because of the frozen ground. Prevention is much easier than cure, so do not allow these conditions to arise. Some sort of exercise is always possible. The horse's diet should be stopped immediately once the horse cannot be exercised, and bran mashes should be given with the necessary dietary minerals. Exercise, even if it is being led round the stable yard for several hours, *must* be implemented.

Azoturia is intensely painful, often fatal and is caused by a concentration of lactic acid in the tissues due to the very rich feed a horse receives when in full work. It has similarities to a very bad case of tying up or founder. A horse which is receiving the correct minerals is not so likely to succumb.

Hosing down the horse's quarters and over the kidneys with cold water after exertion closes the pores too quickly and can also exacerbate the problem. Perhaps the racing trainers of my youth who totally banned water, except for washing feet, knew something! I often wonder why human athletes are not subjected to this nonsense and yet horses are. It is also essential never to feed a horse beyond its requirements and to make sure if it is being highly fed, that the exercise it gets is sufficient to use up all the feed.

Big head, buffel head, NSH (nutritional secondary hyperparathyroidism)

This condition is induced by grazing tropical-type grasses.

In the mid 1900s, this was also known as osteoporosis, and I guess it is not entirely incorrect. It is induced by the horses being unable to get the nutrients they need to keep their facial (and other bones) healthy.

Grass	Total Oxalate	Ca intake Total oxalate	Ca Balance	Estimated true Ca digestibility
Non-hazardous:				
Flinders	0.25	1.92	10.0	99
Rhodes	0.45	1.79	46.1	76
Hazardous:				
Pangola	0.92	0.17	5.7	39
Green panic/				
guinea grass	0.81	0.32	-9.7	42
Para	0.75	0.29	-13.4	24
Kikuyu	1.30	0.23	-22.4	20
Buffel	1.42	0.22	-22.6	16
Narok setaria	1.81	0.15	-14.2	32
Kazungula				
setaria	2.82	0.97	-30.3	3

Ca = Calcium

Paramatta grass bears similarities to the grasses contained in this table.

The above chart shows that there are only two safe African-type grasses. Horses should not have to graze pastures with the other grasses in them. The information in this section is taken from a paper by Dr R A Mackenzie from the Queensland Department of Primary Industries. I had already been asked by several Queenslanders what caused this and allied conditions and suggested they supplement the horses with dolomite/seaweed licks. Improvement was reported and the accompanying information confirms the treatment. These grasses contain amounts of oxalates that totally inhibit calcium and iodine; this will eventually kill a horse (or any other animal) if they graze nothing else. In the experimental work that was done, magnesium levels did not appear to be affected.

Initially, horses become stiff in their gait, then joints swell and breakdowns can occur. They swell along the teeth and jaw area and eventually the whole head becomes swollen; their condition gets very poor, as they cannot eat much. The condition is reported to take two to five months to become evident, and obviously prevention is better than cure. The parathyroid gland is also affected in cases that have been studied at post mortem. Pregnant and lactating mares are at high risk, and this is emphasised in the report.

I had assumed that this disease was incurable. When I met Ross Mackenzie in Queensland we discussed this and he said recovery was possible, provided the bones had not disintegrated. It is therefore a curable condition and is certainly avoidable.

This is yet another illness that highlights the necessity of making dolomite and seaweed freely available in some form. Horses that are most affected are often station horses that are not handfed. Owners of horses that receive their minerals in daily feeds would hardly know that this condition exists. Badly affected horses were found to not take enough of the calcium provided if it was on its own, so molasses was added. However, calcium carbonate on its own is not a safe feed for any length of time, nor is molasses. I therefore recommend a mixture of seaweed meal and dolomite (which has been effective).

NOTE: Big head can affect stud males of other species, not just horses.

Blackleg (clostridium feseri, chauvoei, bacillus chauvoei and B anthracis symtomatis)

This disease is reputed only to affect ruminants, however when I was curing a young goat in 1996, a friend told me her sister's stallion in Queensland had just died from blackleg.

Blackleg is caused by an organism gaining entry by a scratch or surface wound, which has not been disinfected properly, often on old sheep country. Often the original wound is not even seen. Also, a wound must be disinfected *once* properly, as disinfecting more than once can inhibit healing. The vets I first worked with used peroxide, iodine, disinfectant (Lysol in those days) and said if all else fails use alcohol — gin or whisky can be used (a ten per cent copper sulphate solution is also very effective). This disinfectant must be syringed into the wound if necessary and all dirt removed.

With this ailment, the limb, which is usually a rear one, swells to grotesque proportions and the beast is in great pain. Inject 50 ml vitamin C straight into the affected limb repeatedly (every few hours), and give good supportive nursing. As soon as it is eating again, give three or four tablespoons a day of sodium ascorbate powder in the feed, until it is over the worst. Continue to inject the affected limb with vitamin C until it goes down (about twenty-four hours). Find and disinfect the cause if possible.

It would be a good idea to give intravenous vitamin C, B12 and VAM once the horse is stabilised. Do *not* give any injections into the main part of the body before then, as the whole body is intensely sensitised with this disease. The injection (except in the affected limb) will hurt too much. If arnica is available, it is a great idea (orally).

Bleeders, see broken blood vessels

Blindness from capeweed (arctotheca calendula)

This does occasionally happen, even without the usual string-halt occurring first. At the first sign, remove the horse from grazing the weed at once, otherwise permanent blindness will result (it has done so in several cases). Give all the minerals on a daily basis for at least a week, and make seaweed meal freely available. Give 5000 mcg of magnesium orotate daily for a week (crush the 400 mg tablets which are available from health shops and made by Bioglan). Then cut out the extras and feed normally. Give at least 5–10 ml of cod-liver oil by mouth daily for a short time. Get the offending paddock analysed and remineralised at once.

Bog spavin

This is a large lump which comes up just below the hock, generally on the inside, and can be almost the size of a grapefruit in some cases. It does not occur in animals that have been and are receiving all the minerals that I list for soundness. A very bad sprain might bring one up, but I have seen them mainly on horses who are not getting road work or the correct feed. It will gradually flatten out and become hard; emu oil rubbed on lightly could help. Take the horse off heavy work until the lump spreads out and hardens.

Like curb, there is possibly a conformation link.

Bone infections

A horse's leg became badly infected after a needle from an injection hit the bone. After much trauma and trialling of different drugs the vet suggested the horse be put down. The condition that had required the injection was a form of breakdown, and he felt that there was nothing more that could be done.

The horse was nine years old and was given 30 g of sodium ascorbate, 10 ml of vitamin A, D and E powder, dolomite, sulphur and seaweed meal in his feed daily. After a few days the infection started to clear up, and for the first time in two months the healing process was working again. He regained his soundness and was run exactly two months after starting the treatment. Sadly, and possibly predictably, the condition that started the treatment in the first place recurred and he had to be put down. However, the owners were adamant that the treatment suggested had totally cured the horse's infected leg and his resulting lameness.

Occasionally, it is worth trying natural remedies in the face of all odds, especially when conventional ones have not worked.

Bots

Bots lay their eggs on the hairs of the neck, legs and shoulder, anywhere that the horse can reach to bite itself. The eggs are then swallowed and grow in the stomach to a bot of a centimetre or so in length. One bot is not too much of a problem, but there are always large numbers and in post mortem they have sometimes been found occupying up to two-thirds or more of the stomach area. They are passed out when mature, then hatch into more bot flies, and the cycle starts again.

Horses receiving the correct amount of copper and other minerals do not have trouble with bots, and in most cases they do not even lay the eggs at all.

Rubbing the areas where the eggs are likely to be laid with a rag that has been rung out in kerosene is helpful. Another remedy which works well is to increase the cider vinegar in the feed. It is not known whether this deters the flies or kills the bots in the stomach. Both of these remedies seem to be effective and preferable to the drenches available for bots, which are all rather powerful. Some of these are not safe for pregnant mares. For horses that are getting *all* their minerals, however, and are on remineralised land, bots should not be a problem.

Botulism

If this is suspected, drench three tablespoons of sodium ascorbate vitamin C powder by mouth (60 g) and give intravenous vitamin C (at least 40 ml at a time), and repeat until the horse is feeling better. A tablespoon of dolomite and sodium ascorbate powder at a time should be given straight into the mouth as well. Injections of B12 and VAM 10 ml of each should also be given until the appetite returns to normal.

In 1996, there were about twelve cases of botulism in thoroughbreds training in northern New South Wales. Four died before their owners contacted me; the rest were saved. *But*, in spite of the fact that they came from different racing yards and were fed different brands of feed, the feeds had one factor in common, they were all extruded (pelleted). Evidently someone had been supplying very low grade mould-affected material to the various pellet makers. There is *no* way of knowing when this has happened, so make up your own feeds from material you can examine first.

Breakdown

In its severest form, this occurs in the flexor tendon at the back of the front leg from the knee to the pastern. The tendon gives way and the pastern rests on the ground. However, there is nearly always prior warning of strain by heat in the tendon or swelling. The horse must be taken out of work immediately and the vet called. These days there are treatments less radical than the old-fashioned firing for helping this condition. Firing may have produced a sound horse in the end, but the horse's action was never the same again.

If time is no object, even the worst breakdown will heal without treatment if the horse is turned out for eighteen

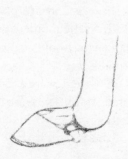

Partial breakdown   Complete breakdown

months. Care must be taken that it gets at least one small feed a day with *all* the minerals it needs, which will help make the repair permanent, and that the paddock is healthy.

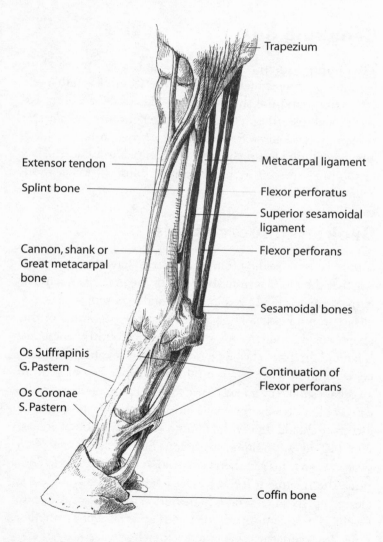

Tendons and ligaments of the foreleg

However, not everyone can wait eighteen months. Nowadays there are new and more successful treatments for breakdown. Electric therapy figures largely and seems to be producing good results. Your vet will be able to advise you.

Breaking out

This happens when the horse is being fed more than it requires. Sometimes this takes the form of small spots, especially round the shoulder and saddle area. Feeding sea-weed meal instead of letting the horse consume the amount it requires has been a frequent cause of this problem (this is why I emphasise letting horses help themselves). Lucerne hay or too much protein-rich feed can all cause it on occasion. Remove the cause.

Broken blood vessels

If the horse is bleeding from the nostrils, have the vet check whether the blood is from the lungs or the membranes; usually the former is bright red in colour and very profuse, but not always in mild cases. The paragraph at the beginning of this chapter offers one reason for the frequency of this complaint. If butazolidin has to be given (and serious thought should precede its administration), a tablespoon per day of sodium ascorbate should be added to the food at the same time. In the case of blood vessels that have already ruptured, the course of ascorbate should start with an intravenous injection of at least 25 g (50 ml) of sodium ascorbate. There is no danger of an overdose, and this can then be halved. It would be wise to continue the treatment for at least a week after the trouble has cleared up. Extra vitamin E in the ration would also accelerate healing. Find a homeopath to provide arnica if ever a painkiller is needed again; the usual potency for a horse is 200 c.

Bruises

Cider vinegar will reduce swellings from sprains and bruises quite quickly. A pad, such as a gamgee (a cotton wool roll, with both sides enclosed in gauze), should be soaked in the vinegar and bandaged lightly onto the affected part. A piece of plastic film is then placed between the pad and the bandage, which should not be too tight. The horse must be rested until the bruise is fully resolved. Any of Dr Jarvis's books on cider vinegar are worth reading. I thought they were rather amusing at first, but soon learned to take them seriously.

Emu oil is another good resource to wipe on bruised areas. It has cleared up bad bruises quite quickly.

Cancer

This condition seems to get more prevalent by the day. Grey horses (and therefore chestnuts, which are genetically linked in colour) are more prone to it than other colours as a rule. Tesio, the great Italian racehorse breeder (of the mighty Ribot), wrote an excellent thesis on the subject and makes a very clear case for grey being a faulty color and a form of melanoma.

If grey horses are kept on healthy remineralised pastures with *no* artificial fertilisers, as well as the necessary minerals in their feed, they do not succumb to cancer. But the tendency is there. Unfortunately, all colours of horse get cancer now.

Administering vitamin C along with a bland and healthy diet, which excludes grains at first *and* keeping a horse on a remineralised paddock can work wonders. The horse should be given a course of intravenous vitamin C; I recommend about 25 g a day (this vitamin is usually sold in 2 ml to a gram mixtures). This should be augmented by oral doses of sodium ascorbate (four tablespoons per day). Vitamin C has great tumour-reduction properties. Extra cod-liver oil or vitamins A and D (about a teaspoon of each daily) should also be given plus all the minerals mentioned in earlier chapters. Tumours usually go down in six weeks, and very occasionally reduce in size in a shorter time. The one exception to this is cancer of the penis and it is probably kinder to euthanase the horse; it is very difficult to get vitamin C to this appendage (or to an udder). However, washing that organ in a mixture of rain-water and a solution of six per cent peroxide (5 ml) in half a litre of water is well worth trying. There have been some interesting cures.

> NOTE: The great French veterinarian Andre Voisin states unequivocally that cancer and insufficient copper in the diet go hand in hand in Soil, Grass and Cancer (see Bibliography).

Coccidiosis

Horses and other animals on the correct minerals do not get coccidiosis, as evidently coccidia do not like copper any more than worms do. This was to me one of the major benefits that came with feeding stock properly. Coccidiosis just did not happen any more.

Blood in the manure and general ill-thrift would be a possible sign of an infection. Have the vet take a test and supply the necessary drugs immediately. The convalescence is long and taxing to the horse keeper, and a very bland diet with food that does not irritate the intestinal linings should be fed. Feeding good, green grass, soft hay, chopped vegetables of all kinds, including beetroot which is especially good, and the addition of eggs and milk to the diet will also help. Mallow leaves are specifically useful against coccidia, and could be added chopped to a little soft lucerne chaff in a daily feed. All forms of hard feed, especially bran and chaffs which can scratch the insides of the intestines, must be avoided until the horse is completely on the mend. The horse must be brought back into work very slowly and carefully once it has recovered.

I cured a very bad case of this in the south of England years ago; the vet had no drugs, but made me feed it just as described. Fortunately, being England, green grass was available in the paddock, which helped. Vitamin E should be given regularly until the horse is fully recovered; give as per the directions on the container. This is another disease that seems to belong to the past. When all stock get their correct minerals, and copper in particular, it does not figure, thank goodness. The remedies nowadays are expensive and can be severe.

Colic

Colic is usually caused by bad feed, a recent application of phosphatic fertilisers, or an imbalance of some sort in the diet, including illegal binges from the feed bin. Make up a drench of four tablespoons of vitamin C (sodium ascorbate), and give immediately. Give 25 cc by injection straight into the muscle on each side of the neck as well. It is not often necessary to repeat the treatment, but it can be given every half hour if necessary. Keep the patient warm and quiet and remove the cause of the trouble. Occasionally colic can be caused by impaction (constipation), and a drench of half a litre of warm cooking oil (not soya or liquid paraffin) is worth trying as well as the vitamin C.

If the colic is caused by mouldy hay, an injection of vitamin B1 should be given as well; consult the vitamin B1 section for amounts. Whatever the cause, colic should be treated as fast as possible; the next stage can be peritonitis or twisted gut, both of which are often fatal.

I was rung early one morning about an aged thoroughbred with bad colic. I asked the owner to ring me once the horse had stabilised following its treatment, as I wished to know what had caused it. I discovered that the rented paddock in which the horse lived had been top-dressed with super-phosphate four days previously. When I told the owner that it was the cause she was most indignant and rang the Department of Agriculture to check. They confirmed what I had said. It could just as well have been amounts of lime that were too high. Horses should not be left in paddocks that are to be conventionally top-dressed or are to have more than a tonne to the acre of lime put on them, as trouble could follow.

Colitis X

This is a rather fancy name for a condition caused by an acute mineral deficiency. It often occurs in horses that have been moved from good pasture to one lacking in nutrients. In the United States and Australia, it has arisen particularly in stud horses that are moved from one place to another, where the minerals in the ground are not the same. It is always fatal if not treated quickly. Always check a horse's gum colour when it is ill; in this condition, they go pillarbox scarlet. Dr Bill Rees, an English vet working at the University of Melbourne in the early 1970s, saved the life of a mare and her foal that was seven months in utero. He taught me the basics.

Usually large amounts of mineral and vitamin-rich intra-venous fluids are given. The horse will be listless and dehydrated, and the gums and tongue bright scarlet. Call a vet immediately, who will give the necessary intravenous fluids. Vitamin B12 and VAM by injection will also help. It is important to get the horse onto its seaweed and feed containing the correct minerals as soon as possible.

Contracted tendons (knuckle-over)

This complaint afflicts newborn foals. The legs of the foal will be bent up or twisted, so the foal, if it can walk, does so on the tips of its hooves. A tablespoon (20 ml) of cod-liver oil by drench should alleviate the condition quite fast. The foal is deficient in vitamins A and D, and probably its mother was too. Both their diets should be amended to provide an adequate supply.

This condition is *not* hereditary and does *not* merit destroying the foal (as is frequently done); it is easily and quickly cured, and even more easily prevented.

Crib biting, see fence chewing and windsucking

Curb

This is a bony swelling each side of and just below the hock. It is associated with bad conformation and can cause lameness, eventually making the horse useless for any sort of riding. In its mild state, if the horse is not being worked too hard, it will not cause too much inconvenience. Bring the horse into work carefully and it may stay sound enough for light work.

Young horses will often develop curbs, which will disappear after a few months' rest and correct nutrition. The latter is the real answer, unless there is a congenital malformation that would predispose the horse to form a curb.

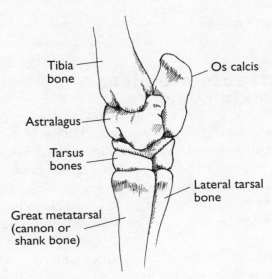

Tibia bone

Os calcis

Astralagus

Tarsus bones

Lateral tarsal bone

Great metatarsal (cannon or shank bone)

Bones of the hock

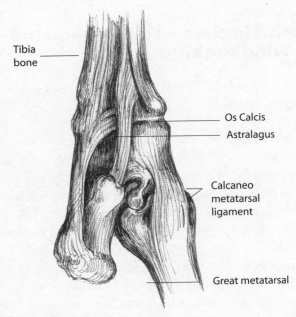

Tibia bone

Os Calcis

Astralagus

Calcaneo metatarsal ligament

Great metatarsal

Ligaments of the hock

Diarrhoea

This disease is sometimes due to worm infestation, but more often due to an imbalance in the feed.

In foals under three months of age, it is nearly always due to a lack of magnesium in the food chain, either from the paddock or the hand feed. However, the most likely cause in older foals and horses is a lack of copper. Hungerford, in his book *Diseases of Livestock*, states that it is nearly always due to a lack of copper in the food chain, and just getting that mineral is enough to stop the ailment.

If it is severe, add one or two tablespoons a day of sodium ascorbate to the diet according to age. In really bad cases, an injection of about 15 ml (7.5 g) of sodium ascorbate can be given as well. Try to ascertain the cause. Is it too much capeweed, sour paddocks or some other problem?

I was lent an Apaloosa mare that had scoured most of her life. She was very picky about eating her feed (and the copper sulphate in it). However, my paddock had been remineralised before her arrival, and the copper content had risen as the other minerals were replaced from 0.2 to 8 ppm. It took six months, but the mare's tail was clean for the first time in her life and her diarrhoea ceased. She also came into season properly, which had never happened before.

Equine coital exanthema (ECE) and equine herpes virus (EHV)

A short time after the stallion has served the mare, pustules and vesicles sometimes appear on the breeding apparatus of both animals. Sometimes the results are serious, other times they clear up in two or three weeks. Veterinary attention must be sought immediately.

Large doses of vitamins C, E and some VAM will help,

and see that the mare is receiving *all* the necessary minerals in her food, especially the copper.

Herpes complaints like a copper-deficient host and are only present when copper is not. Many of the complaints that have surfaced in recent times are due to a lack of copper.

I feel this condition goes back to the basic wellbeing of animals; both stallions and mares should be on the correct vitamins and minerals (especially copper) in their feed and in healthy yards or paddocks. All herpes conditions seem to be present only when the copper levels are incorrect. In fact, the disease does not appear on properly supplemented beasts — whatever the kind.

I also feel that the practice of scoping, unless carried out with *faultless hygiene*, could contribute to the present outbreak of odd venereal conditions. I have seen it being performed without the proper procedures being followed. This is most unwise.

Equine infectious anaemia (EIA)

This is sometimes referred to as equine infectious haemolytic anaemia, swamp fever (in the United States) or horse AIDS.

The disease is diagnosed by a Coggins Test or C-ELISA test; both are available here. The latter has been used for goats for the last twenty years to diagnose their particular form of auto-immune disease.

I had hoped that a section on this auto-immune disease in horses would not be necessary in this book, as it did not appear to have reached Australia. However, by September 1991, four cases had been reported in Western Australia, and since then, cases have been reported in all states.

I am indebted to an article in *The Western Horseman* in November 1989 by Genie Stewart Spears. Spears wrote it under the auspices of Dr C J Issel of Louisiana State University who has researched EIA. The article has the title 'EIA: The Death Warrant'.

Like all auto-immune diseases, there is no known cure for this condition, and all mammal life now appear to have their own particular type. I spent many years with a milking goat herd eradicating the goat variety, a task made easier by pasteurising the milk which would otherwise spread the disease. It can also be spread by blood transfer, but this did not arise in this situation. It was still a soul-destroying process.

EIA (the horse variety) appears to be spread by blood transfer alone, and specifically, by insects that bite or unsterilised injection needles. Horse flies are believed to be the main culprits in the United States, and mosquitoes are not considered to be so dangerous. Feeding a horse the correct amounts of sulphur and avoiding molasses in the feed would help prevent the condition.

Intermittent fever, anaemia, weakness, loss of weight and oedematous swellings under the belly can all be signs of the disease. Spears's article compares it to AIDS, where a lack of immunity means the horse has no resistance to any infection. Some horses, like a few of the goats we had with CAE, can be positive for EIA and show no signs, but they are *carriers*, and can transmit the disease if bitten by the appropriate insect. Foals can be born to affected mares and if they are born EIA-free (not having been infected in utero, which is possible), they can safely suckle the mare, provided there are no biting insects around.

There is no known preventative or cure. However, we do have a preventative which cattle owners have found most successful against an insect-borne disease — bovine ephemeral fever. Cattle receiving sulphur supplementation are not bitten by the carrying insect (believed to be a mosquito), and therefore do not contract the disease. It is quite easy, as suggested in other parts of this book (and above), to supplement your horse regularly with sulphur. A tablespoon per day of milling sulphur powder in its feed will stop insect bites. Sulphur is safe according to the CSIRO as long as it does not exceed two per cent of an animal's whole daily feed intake.

The other factor which is now being recognised is the link between a lack of copper and a high incidence of auto-immune disease. With goat CAE this is a definite factor, and in herds where copper supplementation is inadequate, the disease is prevalent. St John's Wort, which is a plant very high in copper, is now being used in the treatment of AIDS patients, particularly in the United States. In the same context, in the United States it has been found that the copper levels in the human population are now well below the recommended RDA levels (mainly due to plastic plumbing). This is now being cited as a factor in the rapid spread of AIDS. Therefore, it is imperative that horses have access to seaweed meal, *and* that their copper requirements are fully met. Prevention is our only hope. The disease is serious in some parts of the United States, and it would be disastrous to see it develop more than it already has in Australia.

Equine polysaccharide storage myopathy (EPSM)

This is a *new* muscle disease in draughthorses. Beth Valentine from Oregon State University has published a paper on the subject in 1999 and the emphasis is hers.

In brief, EPSM covers many diseases that we have known for years. These include tying up, Monday morning disease, shivers and other abnormal hind limb gaits. The old azotorea is not included, but is obviously in the same category. Valentine implies they are mismanagement states and occur on heavy grain feeding, causing muscle damage and worse.

She also says they seem to affect draught breeds the most and have probably been with us for hundreds of years.

I would also suggest that a draught or heavy horse that is not fed huge amounts of grain at any time (particularly on its day off), and that receives *all* the necessary minerals (with a special emphasis on magnesium), and whose hay and pasture is grown on remineralised soils, will *not* suffer from this condition.

Prevention is definitely better than cure and involves giving magnesium orotate orally (80 mg at a time initially), sodium ascorbate (30 ml in each side of the neck) by injection, and making sure the horse has access to seaweed meal and *all* its dietary minerals — particularly copper sulphate.

Equine protozoal myeloenchephalitis (EPM)

As the name implies, this is a protozoal disease. In the 1960s, when it was first observed in the United States, the infection usually came from contaminated opossum faeces. The actual protozoa was not at first recognised, and in fact, it was deemed to be very similar to toxoplasmosis. The treatment used then and now was fairly radical and some very powerful drugs were used.

What was not recognised then is what we have now found with other protozoal diseases (such as coccidiosis, which was a scourge of all livestock at one time), that is, once we got the copper levels correct in the diets of all animals these diseases did not figure. Prevention is better than cure, as always!

Fence chewing (and stripping bark off trees)

This is caused by the horse looking for nutrients missing from either its paddock or stable feed, copper in particular.

Putting out seaweed on demand, and making sure the horse gets a small meal daily with a teaspoon of copper sulphate (5 g), as well as the dolomite and sulphur, will stop the mayhem. It will be noticed that blacks and chestnuts seem to be the worst offenders, and the copper requirements of these two colours appear to be similar. It is necessary for all adult horses of all colours to be given a teaspoon of copper sulphate daily, as well as the minerals listed in this book.

Fistulous wither (poll evil is a similar condition)

This, like poll evil, is usually caused by the brucella abortus organism. It possibly gains entry from a small sore and, instead of clearing up normally, becomes a large abscessed wound. The sore is usually from an ill-fitting rug or saddle rubbing (or the horse banging its head on a low roof or branch in the case of poll evil). But unless the brucella abortus bacteria is present it should not go much further. This is a zoonose so care must be taken that the operator does not have cuts on the hands when handling or cleaning out the wound. A zoonose is a disease that can be transmitted from animals to human beings.

A vet should be called immediately. If the condition is allowed to become serious the horse will be out of action for quite a while and will possibly ultimately die. This was the first operation that I helped a vet perform and it is strictly not for the squeamish. The horse had an advanced case and we removed over a litre of putrid material from just below the wither. Vitamin C, administered both orally and by injection, will help control the infection, which should be treated initially by syringing the wound with a ten per cent copper sulphate and water solution, as used for Queensland itch and similar conditions. Nowadays, I would suggest trying 10 ml of six per cent peroxide in half a litre of water as a disinfecting agent — it is old, but very effective.

> NOTE: *The brucella organism likes a mineral-deficient host. In the United States, the necessary minerals are copper, cobalt, iodine and manganese (all found in seaweed). In Australia, one would add the lime minerals to this list as well. In other words, a properly fed and cared for equine should not contract it.*

Foot problems

Foot problems that are due to bad diet can show up as misshapen hooves or walls that do not look healthy. These are often only a degree off the laminae becoming inflamed. In fact, a horse's general health for the last six months or so is often apparent in its feet. Giving seaweed (free-take) is the fastest treatment I have seen for restoring hoof growth as well as general health. The biotin in the seaweed is much more effective than the artificial variety that can be bought separately. Make sure that the horse receives its copper and other mineral requirements.

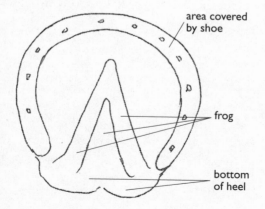

area covered by shoe

frog

bottom of heel

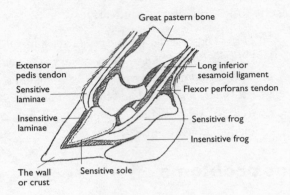

Section of a foot

Forging

This is the name given to the clicking noise made when a horse's back shoes clip the front ones as it moves. Call in a good farrier at once to remedy the shoeing. Occasionally, forging is caused by an unfit horse being too tired to place its feet correctly or it can occur in a horse that is young and/or unbalanced, but the farrier should check in any case.

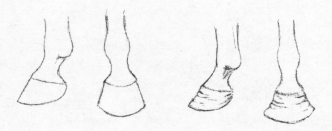

Normal feet   Feet showing ridges due to malnutrition

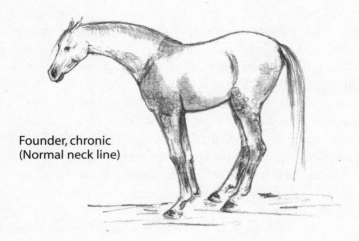

Founder, chronic
(Normal neck line)

Founder

This is caused by an excess of phosphates without the
balancing calcium and magnesium in the diet. This makes
the horse acutely deficient in these minerals.

In chronic cases, the horse will have large areas of hardening round the neck. This will form a crest, and will also
appear across the top of the tail, and in serious cases down the
shoulder (this is sometimes called shoulder founder and considered fatal). This hard tissue is not to be confused with fat,
which should be soft. One cannot stick one's fingers into a
foundered horse; if a depression is made it usually stays for a
few seconds.

In sudden attacks of founder, the feet may get hot and the
horse will have tremors passing down its legs. It will be
unwilling to move and will try to alleviate the pain by standing with all its feet bunched together underneath it. The
treatment is the same in all cases. The sudden attacks will
diminish very quickly, but the chronic build-up of tissue may
take weeks or months to cure according to how long it took

to build up. Regular exercise and a sensible diet is essential.

For sudden severe attacks, give 1 kg of Epsom salts (magnesium sulphate) by drench, dissolved in as little water as possible. If there is a stream nearby, stand the horse in it until the inflammation and pain is reduced. For cases where the feet are no longer inflamed, steady exercise will help to dissipate the magnesium around the tissues.

For chronic cases, give a tablespoon of Epsom salts daily for the first three or four days only, and a tablespoon of dolomite in the feed. The other necessary minerals should be fed as well. The feed, which should contain no grain, should only be large enough to contain all the minerals.

In all cases of founder, it is essential to remove the cause of the ailment, which is invariably feed too low in magnesium or too high in phosphates. The main cause in Australia is poor paddocks. These are paddocks that have possibly been superphospated, and thus have locked up what little magnesium is available, or paddocks with very poor pasture, low pH and poor lime mineral levels. Capeweed and Smooth cat's ear usually proliferate in these conditions. Lucerne hay is also often the cause, and only good pasture hay should be used.

A pony in perfect health was tethered for an hour on grass growing where the superphospate-spreading trucks were washed. It developed founder within four hours. Both front feet were sore and hot, and the front legs had tremors running down them. Two doses, an hour apart, of half a kilogram of Epsom salts by drench had it well on the road to recovery. Make sure that the ex-patient is on all the right minerals.

Superphosphate ties up 5 kg of magnesium to the hectare, according to Peter Bennett, writing in the *Ecologist*. It also renders magnesium unobtainable or inert in the body and drains the system of that mineral. Copper is rendered unavailable by this fertiliser, as well as by urea or any other nitrogenous top dressings. The horse will also be placed at risk because of a low or non-functioning immune system (see section on copper).

Laminitis

This is very similar to founder, and horses that are overfed with too much high protein food without enough exercise to use it up are the main victims.

This is very frequent in the racing industry. Most horses do not get the regular slow conditioning work that *all* horses once received. Laminitis was virtually unheard of then. Nowadays, many horses in the racing industry are on permanent drugs to prevent it!

The laminae, which is the layer inside the hoof wall, will become inflamed, restricting the horse's movement and causing pain. The modern answer is a vaccination or an antibiotic! Changing the exercise regime once the horse is sound again and instituting the measures suggested in the section on founder will provide a cure.

You should reduce the protein in the horse's diet at once and always be present when the farrier checks a new horse. As the foot is cleaned up and extra hoof pared away, the laminae will appear bright pink. This is the first danger sign.

Shelley feet

This is often considered to be a hereditary problem, but it would partly appear to be another case of dietary imbalance. Removing all lucerne from the diet often enables the feet to recover. This means not even lucerne chaff should be used. This course of action is probably a good idea for most foot problems.

When reintroducing the lucerne to the diet, only do so after the horse has been away from it for a while. When reintroducing it, watch the feet carefully. Always employ a good farrier and take his advice.

Venice turps applied outside the foot has a reputation for hardening it up. Equestrians tell me that even cases suffering badly from shelley foot do improve with a good diet!

Genital tract infections, see also urinary tract infections

These should not occur in healthy mares. The cause is similar to that of urinary tract infections. Vitamin A is the most important factor in the health of the genital tract; often, a course of this vitamin on its own will clear up quite stubborn cases and extra vitamin C (as above) should also be given. Any mare that has had this complaint should be swabbed before going to the stallion, as occasionally there is an organism (often corynebacteria) involved, and this can be transmitted to the stallion and thence to other mares.

Drugs are not always the answer; proper minerals in the feed, regular cod-liver oil in the diet, and a healthy, remineralised paddock will usually clear up the condition. Extra vitamin C and vitamins A and D (cod-liver oil) should be given.

Gutteral pouch infection

The gutteral pouch is behind the eyes. The first case I heard of was in a thoroughbred that unusually, according to the owner's vet, had the infection in both sides of its head. The poison from the abscesses paralysed both the larynx and connections to the ears. The result was an excessively nervous horse apparently unable to stand still and circling ceaselessly the whole time. A side effect of the disease was that the poison from the abscesses was eroding the artery walls and causing massive outbursts of nasal bleeding. On one occasion, the horse bled so badly after being at the track that its life was at risk for three days.

The operation to clear the passages and pouches has been done in the United States. A success rate of four out of thirty-one is quoted, and in the 1980s the operation had an estimated cost of between $7000 and $15,000. The owner felt that the operation was out of the question and was considering having the horse destroyed. It was suggested that he give the horse away or run it through the sales. He refused to do this, as he felt it was wrong to let someone else have an animal in that state. The horse was losing condition rapidly, and none of the measures usually tried made any difference. When in a spelling yard, he walked constantly, and in the box, he churned the straw up round the walls until the floor was bare.

After a telephone conversation, the owner agreed to try vitamin and mineral therapy on the animal, having nothing to lose. He gave the animal 60 g (three tablespoons) a day of sodium ascorbate in its feed for the first few days, then cut this down to 20 g daily. He also gave the horse twenty ground-up silica tablets in its feed each day, as these are great blood purifiers. A daily tablespoon, each, of dolomite and seaweed meal were the other additions to the diet. The seaweed would now be given freely, as this is the best way to do it.

He said that after a few days the transformation in the horse was dramatic; it ceased to walk the box and its nervous behaviour had vastly improved. It started to eat hay again, which it had refused to do while ill, and the straw in its box was hardly disturbed during the day. The owner now felt that he would be able to pass the horse on to someone for eventing or similar if the improvement could be maintained. When it was last heard of, all was well, and it had settled into its new home.

NOTE: *This happened twenty-five years ago when intravenous vitamin C was not so easily obtained; now we would use it as well and this would probably speed up the recovery.*

Haemorrhages

Call the vet immediately if a large haemorrhage occurs. If an internal haemorrhage is suspected, examine the mucous membranes, and particularly the gums. A dead, white colour will almost certainly mean there is internal bleeding. For a mild haemorrhage, give a tablespoon of vitamin C in the feed daily to strengthen the smaller blood vessels. Continue the treatment for a few days after the signs of bleeding have stopped. In all cases, a daily B12 and VAM injection at a rate of 10 ml of each in the neck muscle (or vein, if a vet will do it) for two or three days would be of help.

Where there is a large haematoma, do not interfere with it. Give 40 to 50 ml of vitamin C by injection, and powder in the feed as well. A young racehorse, terribly injured in a smash with a car, had a haematoma from her neck to her brisket. Two weeks later, she had normalised on the treatment above (this is the same case mentioned in the section on arnica).

Herpes infections

These usually respond quite well to extra doses of vitamin C and B6. Early on in my dairying days I discovered that animals with herpes infections were also deficient in copper. So horses receiving seaweed meal and correct minerals, including copper, should not contract them.

If there are exterior rashes, these can be washed with a ten per cent copper sulphate solution to dry them up.

Hives

This condition is similar to breaking out, but is usually caused by an allergy. The vet should be able to tell the difference. If it is hives, elevated doses of vitamin C may often be of help.

Allergies usually mean the animal's vitamin C and mineral reserves are lower than they should be.

Dr W A Albrecht has said that allergies are not due to too much of the wrong substances, but to too little of the right minerals to keep the system in order; I have found this to be the case.

Hyperkalaemic partial paralysis (HYPP)

This condition is also documented in humans, but apparently not considered to be hereditary. It certainly is a hereditary condition in horses, therefore this condition should *not* exist, for this reason. It causes horses that are positive with it to suddenly stop, they usually shake and fall very quickly and are thus extremely dangerous to ride.

It can hardly be termed a disease; it is a hereditary condition found in the direct descendants of a very fine quarter horse called Impressive, although he apparently did not suffer from it. It is dangerous, as the sudden paralysis can strike affected horses at any time without warning, and riders have been injured. Like some hereditary diseases it can be carefully bred out, but *all* affected animals or carriers should be destroyed or sterilised. This has not been done yet however, so the condition is still with us.

If a horse positive with the condition is mated to a negative, there is a chance that one foal in two will not have the disease or carry it according to Mendel's Law, *but* this program should not be undertaken unless the breeder is prepared to destroy all positives or carriers.

The disease means that the horse needs to be fed very carefully, as it is excess potassium in the system that causes the fainting effect (excess potassium affects the heart). Those of my clients who have been landed with these horses find that careful supplementation with magnesium orotate has helped control the symptoms (as the magnesium and potassium should be in balance).

Unfortunately, all the horses that have this complaint are, like their progenitor, beautiful specimens. In the United States they may not be exhibited in public, but there are ranches where nearly every horse is positive and the condition is controlled with a drug so that the horses can compete with each other. They are not allowed to compete in public, shows when on the drug.

As salt and potassium are interchangeable, do not feed salt to these animals; let them help themselves.

Immunisation/vaccination reactions

These are a very real problem in performance horses in the United Kingdom where annual equine influenza immunisations in the racing industry are mandatory. These cause an adverse reaction because they drain the system of vitamin C. If the vitamin C is low due to a lack of greenfeed, an immunisation can occasionally kill. This reaction can be largely stopped by giving at least 25 g (50 ml) of intravenous sodium ascorbate by injection an hour or two prior to the immunisation. Alternatively, two tablespoons daily of sodium ascorbate powder can be administered for three days prior to the immunisation. Read the section on vitamin C in chapter five.

Injuries

All flesh injuries should be well cleaned with disinfectant at once, and then treated with a healing ointment such as comfrey, aloe vera or calendula. Disinfectant should not be used more than once, as it retards the healing process. If the injury is purely cosmetic, use as mild a disinfectant as possible, as this will help prevent permanent scarring. The aim is to promote healing as quickly as possible. Another excellent remedy is to soak a pad in Flint's oils and apply it to the cleaned wound, keeping the pad moist with the oil at all times. Broken knees have been healed without scarring by this method.

Any wound that needs stitching must be attended to immediately; a few hours later is generally too late. It is not fair on the vet to expect a tidy result when the wound has been left several hours and the edges have been allowed to contract and dry. In all wounds, care should be taken to avert tetanus. Tetanus anti-toxin should be given if the horse is not immunised. If unavailable, give the horse about 20 g (a table-spoon) of vitamin C (sodium ascorbate) orally on a daily basis for the next two weeks. Vitamin C (25–50 cc) should be given either intramuscularly or intravenously on the first day. See the section on tetanus.

Johne's disease, often called Crohn's in humans and horses

This disease strikes horses in much the same way as it does other species, including humans.

It is caused by mycobacterium paratuberculosis. The bacteria gets into the wall of the intestines, causing inflammation initially, which then becomes a thickening and callousing of the intestine walls. This means that the horse cannot absorb any nutrients from its feed and dies ultimately from starvation.

Careful nursing and feeding will kill the bacterium and the gut flora will be able to build up again.

The incidence of the disease is basically due to a lack of essential minerals, and it would not occur in a horse on fully remineralised pasture which was getting its dolomite, sulphur, copper sulphate *and* kelp ad lib in its rations, particularly the latter. It should also be getting vitamin A and D (in cod-liver oil) occasionally and cider vinegar in its feed.

To cure it, use large daily doses of injectable vitamin C — 50 ml at a time. This should be accompanied by:

10 ml of vitamin B12;

10 ml of VAM (vitamins, amino acids and minerals in liquid form); and

10 ml of vitamin B15, (DADA).

These should all be given on a daily basis for at least fifteen or sixteen days and can be given intravenously in the same syringe. Feed very light food with *all* the necessary minerals at the same time. Small animals are usually totally cured in ten days. Grazing on really healthy pasture when the horse is well enough would also help.

Knuckle-over, see contracted tendons

Lampas down

Sometimes this condition is called soft palate. The old remedy was to score the top of the mouth with a knife and rub in salt. Rubbing in salt usually works quite well without the mayhem! Again, I have not heard of this condition arising in a properly-supplemented horse.

Leucopenia, lack of leucocytes in peripheral blood

The treatment as suggested for Johne's (Crohn's) disease could only help this condition. Have the vet monitor the blood regularly until the horse is well. Work out the reason for the ill health. Poison sprays certainly contribute to it. In any case of this kind, vitamins A, E, C, B12 and B15 (DADA) and a full complement of the required oral minerals will help.

Lice

Lice are caused by a lack of sulphur in the diet. The use of artificial fertilisers has, according to the CSIRO, inhibited the uptake of sulphur almost totally. Normally it would be obtainable in most grains.

If a horse arrives covered in lice, give it two tablespoons of sulphur daily in its feed for three days, and then cut it back to normal. If they are very bad and causing irritation, give it a wash with a show shampoo the first day, or rub dry sulphur along its back-line, into the bottom of the mane and top of the tail, otherwise the addition of the sulphur in the feed will clear them up in about a week. Once they have all disappeared, feed as normal. (Read the section on sulphur.)

Mastitis

In Australia, dairy cattle and goats that receive supplementary dolomite in their bail feeds are not prone to mastitis, so it is wise to make sure that pregnant and lactating mares also receive their ration. If a mare contracts mastitis despite receiving the correct additives in the feed (particularly her copper ration), lower the protein levels at once. Then remove the grain and/or made-up mixtures from the diet and feed as suggested in the previous chapter on feeding practice.

To overcome the mastitis give her three tablespoons of dolomite and sodium ascorbate powder in her feed daily, until the symptoms ease. In serious cases back this up with 25 cc of vitamin C either in the muscle or vein. Mastitis will clear up very quickly under this treatment and will not leave the udder scarred or damaged. Cut the dolomite back to the usual dose once the udder is back to normal. Make sure the mare is receiving all her minerals. Overseas, farmers have found that a lack of copper also contributes.

For black or septic mastitis, use half a teaspoon (3–4 ml) of hydrogen peroxide in 100 ml of rainwater and insert into the udder as an intra-mammary. Milk the mare out and repeat the next day. This method should work very quickly.

Mouldy corn (maize) poisoning

This was reported in *Acres USA* in February 1995. At the time it was virtually unheard of in Australia, but now it is well-documented. Diseases caused by mouldy corn (maize) have been known in the United States since the turn of the century. Corn poisoning, leukaemia, circling disease and leukoencephalomalacia (Equine ELEM) are the general terms for them. The mould can cause severe and generally fatal neurological disorders. The cause is, as the name says, mouldy corn. Check all feed, not just corn, for black dust, uncharacteristic colours, or a bad smell. Poor storage or growing conditions contribute to the condition. This is a problem for all livestock these days. The remedies do not work and if the horse survives there is often residual and/or hormonal damage. Prevention (as always) is better than cure.

Maize grown on fully remineralised and healthy paddocks would not produce this effect.

Mud fever

This condition can make a horse very sore and lame quite suddenly, and can occur in any colour of horse, but often the white legs are affected the worst or before the others. Little pustules will be seen round the pasterns and the bottom of the legs — in some cases the whole leg swells up. A wash with copper sulphate (thirty per cent solution) will help dry it up and the addition of a teaspoon of copper sulphate to the diet daily will clear it up completely — usually in a day or two. For a very large and heavy horse the copper may have to be doubled.

Amend the diet, and feed as advised in the preceding chapter. Dark-coloured horses and chestnuts are most likely to be afflicted as they need more copper than light-coloured ones. I wish we had known this when working with hunters in the 1950s in the United Kingdom. The suggested remedy then was lead lotion, gallons of it, which we slopped all over their legs (and ourselves) with no effect at all!

Navicular disease

This is a very painful condition inhibiting blood supply to the extremities, causing pain and, if not treated, eventual breakdown of the foot. It appears to be similar to repetitive strain injury (RSI) in human beings and responds to the same treatment.

Firstly remove, if possible, the cause. In the old days, this was a disease that eventually struck down old cab horses after years on the road. This was because they did not receive much in the way of greenfeed (which should contain potassium).

Now, it seems mostly to afflict horses that have been brought into concentrated work in arenas or yards without first hardening up the legs by roadwork (see chapter ten on conditioning). Young quarter horses seem to be the most afflicted.

The old remedy was to unnerve the horse so it could not feel the pain. This was a dangerous practice, as it is extremely difficult to cut the nerve without cutting the blood supply to the foot as well. The lack of blood to the foot would eventually cause it to atrophy and, in extreme cases, drop off, often with little or no warning.

Give the horse about 8000 mcg of vitamin B6, and about the same of potassium phosphate tablets. Both will have to be ground up and added to the feed. Continue daily until recovery is observed. Then amend to the regimen suggested in chapter seven, making sure that the seaweed meal and salt are available on demand and enough cider vinegar (a source of natural potassium) is given daily (250 ml at least).

The horse should only be given light work such as quiet walking on firm ground until the condition eases. The horse owner should review the animal's program to ensure that there is no recurrence.

> NOTE: *Quite a few cases of reported navicular disease in recent times have turned out to be mild pedal bone arthritis and have cleared up very quickly when treated as that disease. It is quite difficult to see a constricted blood vessel on an X-ray especially at the onset of the illness. Borax, as used to cure arthritis, does seem to be beneficial in these cases as well.*

Open knees (epiphysitis)

This is the term for knees that have not knit properly as the foal grows into a yearling. When the foal is small the knees are made of six plates which join together (like the fontanel in a human baby) to make one solid hard bone. This process should be complete by the time the horse is eight months old. In cases of open knees, the bones have not grown together properly, due to an absence of the correct bone-building minerals and the vitamin A and D needed to assimilate them.

If the young horse is fed a ration as suggested in the preceding chapter, the bones should join together in the correct

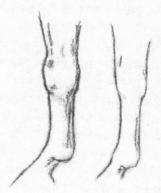

Normally
developed knee

Underdeveloped knee

manner in a few months. Serious work can commence then if
it is old enough. This is curable at any age, no matter how bad.

Over-reach

This happens when the back feet strike into the front legs or
the back of the front feet, and is rather similar to an advanced
stage of forging. Sometimes this is due to bad shoeing, but
more often to the horse being too unfit to do the work
required of it. Call in the farrier and work out remedial action
if bad shoeing is the cause.

In horses hunting or eventing on heavy, holding country,
it can also be due to landing on an overly yielding surface
after a jump, where the front legs do not clear before the back
feet come down.

Whatever the cause, it must be remedied, because if the
horse strikes into the front tendon, breaking down can be the
next stage. Boots and bandages will protect the front legs and
feet to a certain extent, but it is important to remember they
only prevent cutting. They cannot entirely stop bruising.

Years ago, I had a top hunter who struck into the tendon after landing from a jump in deep clay. He sustained quite a sizeable cut, and the vet said this did not affect the tendon — once the cut was healed it would be safe to hunt him again. He was to have steady road work while healing.

I gave him an extra month once the cut was healed and then sent him out hunting, well bandaged. He came back after two hours with the pastern flat on the ground. The bruising had done much more damage than was realised. It is important to consider this possibility when an over-reach occurs. Today, a tendon scan would have picked up the extent of the damage. That horse recovered fully after eighteen months at grass and spent many more useful years as a huntsman's horse, with no trouble whatsoever.

Paniculitis

This is a disease caused by a deficiency of selenium and vitamin E. It manifests as hard, whitish lesions about the size of the palm of the hand on the body area. The affected animal appears mopey and off-colour, with a slightly raised temperature and increased respiration. Cortisone injections were tried on the first case, as the vet suspected a wasp or bee sting, but they only made it worse.

The addition of seaweed meal and minerals, particularly sulphur, to assimilate the selenium in the seaweed meal, is enough to cure the condition in a few days. Consult the sections on selenium, sulphur and vitamin E.

Pinkeye, see sandy blight

Poison bites

The most usual poison bites are from snakes, spiders and ticks.

All three respond equally quickly to massive doses of vitamin C.

The quicker remedial action is taken, the better. The longer the snake or other venom is in the body, the more lasting the damage that may be done.

Snakebite can be detected by examining the eyes if the actual bite is not visible (which it rarely is). The pupils of the patient's eyes will be fully enlarged so that the whole eye appears black. At this stage, the horse may be down, or going down.

Inject 50 ml (25 g) into the muscle on each side of the neck and repeat in an hour's time even if the animal does show signs of recovery. Do *not* waste time trying to give intravenous injections as the veins collapse in shock. By the second injection, the vein will probably be apparent again.

A friend phoned to say her horse was ill, and argued with me that it had not been bitten by a snake. I told her to inject it and she went down to the paddock to prove me wrong by giving the vitamin C in the vein — she could not! But she was able to do so for the second injection, by which time the horse was up again.

Many horses have been saved using less vitamin C than this, even after bites containing large amounts of tigersnake venom. However, excess vitamin C does no harm and excess snake venom is not worth taking a chance on! It is safer to give injections in cases of severe snakebite, as the muscles may be so paralysed that the horse will be unable to swallow an oral dose properly without it going down the windpipe.

Keep the patient warm and comfortable. The advantage of using vitamin C is that the type of snake is immaterial, which is not the case with antivenene, nor is there any danger of anaphylactic shock. A blood test taken by the vet will reveal the type of snake if it is of concern.

Spider bites often do not produce anything more than swellings at the site of the bite. The locality determines the degree of danger. For example, a bite on the throat could cause asphyxiation. Give vitamin C by injection or mouth if the horse can swallow; 20 g (40 cc) daily should be enough, but more can be given if desired. These bites often take several days to go down. Continue the vitamin C in the feed (a tablespoon) until it does.

White-tailed spider bite does not follow the same pattern as other poisonous spider bites. The bite is apparently intensely acid and often is not visible until an enlarged area of necrosis becomes apparent a day or two after it has happened. By this stage it is extremely painful. Make a dressing with either a piece of lint or gamgee, smear it with vaseline or something similar and cover with sodium ascorbate; keep this on the bite until it clears up. This usually takes a few hours. One authority says that ordinary detergent would work the same way. I have not tried this but I have tried the vitamin C method and found it most successful. Give extra vitamin C orally for a few days.

Tick bites produce coma and death. Obviously, it is desirable to start treating the horse as soon as possible, but if it should be found already in a coma, the same amounts of vitamin C as for snakebite can bring it round and effect a recovery. It seems that the longer the tick venom is in the body, the longer the recovery takes. Remove the tick as soon as possible. Applying a dab of tea tree oil on its rear will kill it and make it let go. Apparently, any sort of alcohol will work just as well.

Ticks are a problem in sick, sour, low pH country, and having the paddocks analysed and top-dressed with the required lime minerals will be necessary. If the horse is receiving the correct diet (sulphur included with no molasses), the chances of tick infestation will be lessened.

If a horse is living in country prone to snakes, it is wise to keep several bottles of injectable vitamin C on hand (store in a fridge but do not freeze). Some authorities in the United States suggest a regular maintenance dose of a tablespoon of vitamin C in feed daily as an 'advance backup' in bad snake country. One of the United States' foremost small animal vets suggests a teaspoon a day for dogs going to tick-infested areas. This gives one a little more time when treating the patient.

In all cases of poison bites *if* the bite can be found, rub sodium ascorbate powder into the site as well. It nullifies the pain (which can be considerable) in minutes.

Poisons

Signs of poisoning include foaming at the mouth, a strange smell in the mouth and breath generally, and collapse. If poisoning is suspected, give the horse oral doses of dolomite and vitamin C powder (three tablespoons of each in as little water as possible). Both of these substances have great detoxifying powers. Call the vet as soon as possible and do not give liquids until he gives permission. If it is a case of phosphorus poisoning, this could cause a terrible death. Intramuscular injections of 25 cc of vitamin C would also be a good idea.

If the vet is unavailable, keep the patient quiet and continue the treatment, adding two tablespoons of vitamin E powder, and giving the above dose every three hours. Mix the ingredients with a little milk or egg white; after three doses continue administering vitamins C and E only. If the horse is going to recover, an improvement will be noted within an hour or so of starting the treatment. This should be continued until the horse is a hundred per cent.

In the absence of the vet, an animal with phosphorus poisoning has a sweet smell on the breath (as it does for arsenic), and the patient will show signs of distress and crave water. Its insides are burning and will burn if you let it have water. It takes about thirty-six hours of concentrated nursing to bring an animal through.

The treatment suggested above has saved animals with this type of poisoning.

1080

1080 is 23 ppm sodium fluoride. 1080 poisoning can only be cured in the first twenty minutes after ingestion. Few vets carry the antidote, glycorol mono acetate, as it is difficult to get and rarely needed. The horse will die about four hours later (inevitably) in agony. It should be shot before that happens. The antidote must be given in the first twenty minutes.

The only animal we saved was a dog seen taking the bait. We immediately made it vomit and gave it dolomite, *sodium* ascorbate and a little milk. This managed to neutralise the incredibly severe fluoride acidity.

Arsenic

This poisoning generally leaves residual damage. Large doses of vitamin C and E can help but it is usually a wasted exercise, as the arsenic very quickly causes residual damage, especially to the hormone system. I brought a valuable goat through it as above, but eventually she had to be put down. Make sure this poisoning cannot occur.

Organophosphate and chemical poisoning

Whatever kind, this is very difficult to cure. Administer large and continuing doses of vitamin C, vitamin E, water-based vitamin A (available in tablets to be crushed from a health shop) at about 60,000 units at a time, and zinc in some form. Seaweed meal may possibly effect relief too. Doctors and vets tell me it is the poisoning they dread most, as they feel so helpless. Dr Kalokerinos found the above mixture more effective than anything else, and some alpacas in New Zealand were saved using this method a few years ago.

Proud flesh

This is the term given for the granulations that build up round a wound. They are nature's way of filling it up. When this process continues to the point where it builds up in lumps, it is known as proud flesh. This only occurs in animals that are down on their copper and the remedy is quite simple.

With cases of large lumps — and I have seen photos of one lump bigger than a football on a mare's leg — the following dressing will reduce the lump by about an inch a day. Take some gamgee tissue or similar, soak it in Flint's Oils and spread dry copper sulphate all over the dressing. Wrap this round the proud flesh and hold it on with a bandage.

Repeat until the limb or affected area is quite clean and healthy, then apply Flint's Oils to keep the flies off until the lesion heals and the hair grows. When using copper sulphate in this way, it only destroys putrid tissue; once it gets to sound flesh it may sting but by then the owner should have the wound covered in Flint's Oils or similar. Therefore the final stages of the proud flesh reduction should be carefully monitored.

For small outbreaks, an antiseptic ointment called septicide works quite effectively, but in each case the horse's diet must be amended. Seaweed meal and 5 g (one teaspoon) of copper sulphate *must* be included in the normal diet daily with all the other minerals. This should totally prevent a recurrence.

Queensland itch (known as Canadian itch elsewhere!)

This is caused by a fungus. A wash made up of a tablespoon of copper sulphate, with the same of cider vinegar, dissolved in 500 ml of water and rubbed in well will stop it before it gets going. It is, of course, just another manifestation of a copper deficiency, but is nonetheless extremely contagious among horses that are short of that mineral.

Quittor

This is the name given to a condition where the horse breaks out in running pus round the coronet. It is nearly always due to feeding too much protein without the exercise to use it up. Give the horse a bran mash and put it on plain grass hay or in a paddock with limited feed. Give vitamin C by mouth, three tablespoons a day, until the condition clears up. Care must be taken that the legs and coronet do not become infected. Wash the pus away with a tablespoon of copper sulphate and the same of cider vinegar in 500 ml of water and keep the lesions free of flies with Flint's Oils. It is important that the patient be given its minerals in its chaff and bran and it should *not* be given hard feed for a while.

Rain scald

This was something I had neither seen nor heard of when I wrote the first edition of this book in 1989. Horses at grass without rugs, and sometimes with them, get large, bald patches where the hair will not grow until they are fed properly.

Hair (and wool) needs keratin, and keratin needs copper and sulphur. This was stated categorically in a printout which students for a degree in agriculture had to learn in the 1950s. I am indebted to Bob Crauford of Albury for it.

Rain scald generally occurs in unrugged horses deficient in their minerals that live in cold and rainy areas, but not always. The hair is shed, leaving the skin rough and sore.

My horses had often experienced these conditions without any ill effects, they were on good land, and later always had mineral supplements. Making seaweed meal available to horses has cleared up cases and prevented them from recurring. If a horse was so copper deficient that it was also eating fences the copper suggested for that habit would be needed. Horses at grass should all receive their minerals and have access to seaweed meal whether or not they are being hand fed. A maintenance ration of a small feed containing their minerals twice a week is all many of them need.

Rigs

This is the term for a horse that has not been gelded properly and has one testicle which reappears after a period of time, usually about the fifth year. It can occur because the testicle was missed at the time of gelding, but as most people can count up to two, I have often wondered about that. Vets have told me that they believe it is occasionally the result of a piece of the testicle being left and a new one building up. This generally happens in the wrong place, causing pain and making the horse unpredictable. This makes more sense, as the timespan for a rig to become apparent is generally five years.

Quiet geldings suddenly develop rather wayward behaviour, and can be dangerous in the hands of children. If the scrotum is examined while these bouts are in progress a testicle can often be seen, but the horse will draw it up out of sight very quickly. Operating on a rig is a high-risk proceeding, as the testicle is usually misplaced by that stage.

> NOTE: It is illegal to sell a rig, whether the seller is aware of it or not.

Ringworm

This is not due to a worm, but to a fungus that works in concentric circles, making it look like a worm. Being a fungus, it is therefore another sign of copper deficiency. A wash of twenty per cent copper sulphate in water scrubbed in well will kill the infection. In tender areas, cider vinegar alone, rubbed in several times a day on its own is also effective, but is slower. Give the patient the normal supplements in its diet and it will not recur. This means that the seaweed must be available and the copper in the ration must be the normal 5 g (one teaspoon) per week.

Ross River virus (Ross River fever)

This disease is already well-known, as it occurs in humans and most other stock. It is carried by mosquitoes which have bitten an infected body or carrier. In horses, it only seems to occur in animals not fed their sulphur on a regular basis, that also receive molasses in their rations. Mosquitoes and flies like sulphur-deficient hosts with sugar in their bloodstream; this was reported in *Acres USA* in the late 1970s. One person who rang in with an infected horse had started to feed it molasses about a month previously!

For this reason, I have discouraged the feeding of molasses; the other two diseases spread by biting insects are, if anything, worse — anthrax and EIA (horse AIDS).

To date, curing Ross River virus has been a slow process. Weeks of careful nursing and management with mega doses of vitamin C, 30–40 g intravenously initially and then four tablespoons a day orally in the feed, added to the best mineral feeding possible are required. This has cured the virus in about six weeks. Some of the horses started with 4000 titres of Ross River virus in their blood and were reduced to between two and 300. After this they were quite capable of winning races and several did so, but they were also capable of trans-mitting the illness to horses at risk.

Thanks to Shona Gilbert's endlessly enquiring mind (she is a trainer who has used most of the above methods), a new and very simple remedy derived from Chinese medicine was revived. Half a teaspoon of ground ginger should be administered three times a week for maintenance, and daily for an infected horse. They clear up quite quickly, but ongoing blood tests are necessary. A course of vitamin B15 (DADA), given at a rate of about 7 ml a day would help as Ross River virus can affect the liver.

My farrier used to stay with his grandparents in the Mallee as a child. His grandfather ran teams of dam-sinking Clydesdales. Rod watched him giving them their feed of citrus peelings from the Mildura factories and scattering some powder over it all. He was told this stopped them getting Ross River virus! Vitamin C from the peelings and powdered ginger! This knowledge has been around for over a hundred years!

Two very old therapies recently revived have provided a further breakthough — colloidal silver (which the pharaohs used) and oxygen therapy — using hydrogen peroxide. Both have antibiotic properties and are disease preventatives. Cattle on the 'anthrax belt' received them in the water and survived without incident. Horses that have been put on the treatment, via their water supply, have been tested totally clear of Ross River virus after a course of treatment, but it took too long. Most of the books on these modalities refer to human beings; Ed McCabe's *Oxygen Therapies* (see Bibliography for details) is one. There have been reports in the United States of using colloidal silver for animals. Chlorine no longer figures as a dairy wash or swimming pool disinfectant these days, mixtures of hydrogen peroxide and colloidal silver are a completely safe alternative to chlorine, which has undesirable side effects.

Sandcrack

This is the name for a crack that runs from the top to the bottom of the hoof. It is quite serious and will need remedial

Sandcrack

shoeing, as well as sufficient time for the crack to grow out. Making seaweed freely available would be the best thing, in conjunction with the other minerals already mentioned. Sandcrack was considered to be an inherited condition, so stallions with the ailment were avoided. However, I think it is another of those conditions that are due to inadequate minerals in the diet and environmental factors. Certainly none of the foals from a good Galloway stallion with bad sandcrack I knew ever had it.

Sanding, sand colic

Sanding is not so easy to cure as ordinary colic. Its name denotes that this condition is due to the horse eating too much sand with its food (often in drought conditions). This means there is an appreciable amount of it in the gut impeding correct digestion. Eventually it can reach the stage where a horse could look pregnant if it lives long enough on the reduced nutrients.

In the United States there is a mucilage product on the market that claims to take the sand out with it on the way through the gut. Here, psyllium husks help.

The time-honoured remedy (for lack of any other) was for two people to take a smooth round pole and, standing each side of the horse, lift the abdomen from front to back. A sanded horse will eventually die, so something had to be tried. The above is worth trying and sounds more hopeful.

Another tip worth trying was given to me by one of my Western Australian clients. Years ago, they had a badly sanded horse on the station (Western Australia has predominantly sandy soil). A swagman they had not seen before called in to see if he could stay a few days to be fed and do odd jobs. He saw the horse and remarked that it looked badly sanded. He told them to fetch some unclipped oats, which were fairly usual in those days, and he fed the horse about 2 lb. The sand came through in buckets and after a few days of the therapy the horse recovered. The family has used this method ever since.

It is sad that so many of the old remedies have been allowed to lapse. When I mentioned this story to someone, they remembered being told that chopped-up apples were also effective.

A simple and easy preventative is to give 500 g (three cups) of psyllium husks (obtainable from a health shop) to horses on normal feed. If a lot of sand comes through this may be given again, and can do no harm. Use this method when the pasture is dry and dusty in late summer and early autumn. In a very bad year, it may need to be used more often.

My blacksmith and I tried (unsuccessfully) to revive a pony which collapsed. He put his hand into the mouth and up the anus as far as he could. Each time, the sand came out solid. We realised that there was not really anything we could do, especially as the owners did not like the suggestion that their feed regimen and bad paddocks were responsible.

Sandy blight, pinkeye, conjunctivitis, opthalmia

The eye goes opaque and will ulcerate if not treated. It is only a vitamin A deficiency; fill a 15 ml syringe with cod-liver oil, squirt 3 ml into each eye and the rest into the mouth — this usually works the first time.

Sarcoids

These are tumours, possibly benign, that crop up in or on all parts of the horse. They are becoming far too common. A vet will advise whether removal is practicable or not. Many sarcoids seem to disappear when conditions are improved or changed, without any need for surgical intervention.

In the case of it being inoperable (and the operation is not always successful anyway), a fully balanced diet with *no* made-up feeds or grain, and with all the required minerals will gradually reduce or stop it from becoming worse.

Prevention is better than cure with this complaint as with many others. It seems to occur on horses fed sick food from sick paddocks, and is often accompanied by too much protein in the diet.

Have the horse paddocks remineralised and fully balanced as soon as possible. Never use conventional NPK fertilisers in horse paddocks. Make sure that the horse receives *all* its minerals, especially the copper (see section on cancer), and give extra sodium ascorbate for a while, at the rate of a tablespoon three times a week.

> NOTE: Dr Andre Voisin states that cancer and a lack of copper go together.

Severe combined immune deficiency (SCIDS)

This is a hereditary condition that was first identified in Arab horses in 1973. It is, like most diseases of this nature, a recessive, and took horse owners and vets by surprise initially. Recessives become apparent when two individuals carrying the gene for whatever disease condition are mated. This does not have to be a disease; colour inheritance often works that way too.

If the animal involved is a goat and has four young, Mendel's Law will apply to a point. One will have the disease, one will be totally clear and two will be possible carriers. In goats, this determines whether or not the young will be horned.

Apparently SCIDS was widespread before anyone realised where it came from. Unfortunately, there are breeders who do not understand these manifestations and think if nothing is said they will go away. SCIDS is not dangerous, merely heart-breaking. The foal will look good at first, but quite soon it will start to go downhill, develop skin problems and diarrhoea, and will be dead by the time it is three months old. Nothing arrests the proceedings. The disease is horribly like AIDS-related conditions. It is a blood disorder that cannot be cured.

I have a collection of veterinary papers on this sad condition. Michael Bowling pointed out in 1997 that the 'buck could literally stop there'. By then, it was known where the SCIDS gene was and how to test for it. Previously, nothing was able to pinpoint it. At least one paper implies that ignoring it and just making sure you do not mate two carriers is the way to go! In my view, this would ensure the whole Arab breed and ultimately many others would be carrying a nasty and lethal recessive. This is why Michael Bowling emphasised immediate action to stop the scourge.

Like HYPP (see this chapter), the previous hereditary condition mentioned, the horses and foals carrying SCIDS are especially beautiful. This does not make it any easier. I feel the only way to deal with it is as my local vet suggested for HYPP. In both cases, tests will show which animal has it. If all the carriers were sterilised, the disease would eventually disappear. It seems sad that one of the toughest breeds of horse in the world should have come to this. It is two breeds, if you count quarter horses, which also suffer from HYPP.

Seedy toe

This is often caused by a nail that has pierced the hoof or an abscess that has formed behind the hoof wall. Seedy toe only occurs in horses receiving too little copper. A nail prick in a healthy horse heals up. It will not turn to seedy toe and cause an abscess to form. The best treatment is to use the copper spray as advised for Queensland itch; put it in a syringe and squirt it into the abscess until it is clean. A lump of tow (frayed rope) soaked in Stockholm tar should be kept in the hole until it is clean and healed. Amend the feed at once! Read the section on white line disease.

Shelley feet, see foot problems

Shin soreness

This was definitely something one never heard of in racing in the middle of the century in the United Kingdom, but I gather it has been known in Australia for longer than that. It only seems to happen to horses whose bones have not grown, strengthened and hardened properly. A period on the right feed and minerals usually stops it occurring again. When the bone growth is inadequate the correct anchors for the tendons, muscles and ligaments do not grow as they should either, so the legs are not as strong as they should be. Proper pre-training, which ensures that the legs harden as they should, must be mandatory.

Sidebones

These are bony protuberances that can be felt each side of the foot below the pastern. They can be caused by the horse wearing shoes too high in the heel, which limits the elasticity of the tread.

Depending on how deep-seated they are, they can cause intermittent lameness, particularly on hard ground. Trotters and heavy horses seem to be the most prone to this ailment. Sidebones are not too serious if the horse is only wanted for light work. Many an old horse with sidebones has gone on quietly taking its owner for rides.

The condition is just another result of inadequate feeding which lacks the correct bone-building minerals and vitamins; quite bad sidebones have dispersed over a few weeks like splints. They are amenable to good feeding. Go easy on the grain, make sure there is no lucerne hay and give all the right minerals in the feed.

Snakebite, see poison bites

Spider bite, see poison bites

Spinal problems

These can be caused by the nature of the horse's work. Showjumpers are often most affected. They are required to negotiate high jumps after spreads, and the sudden change of pace causes the vertebrae to be pushed together.

In the United Kingdom about thirty years or so ago, it was found that fusing lumbar vertebrae had to be separated surgically at regular intervals. A nasty kind of operation!

A basic cause of this problem is the degeneration of the disks between the vertebrae. This only occurs when there is inadequate vitamin C for the requirements of the horse, and supplementation by large doses over a period of time has produced excellent results. Doses of 15 g intravenously twice a week have been used most successfully in humans, therefore a horse needs at least twice that amount (remembering that it synthesises its own vitamin C — about 30 g per day — and humans do not). After two to three weeks, the dose could then be given orally in the feed. Recovery usually takes place in a few weeks. At the same time, the diet should be studied to see that the horse is getting the minerals that it needs. The Germans first pioneered this method on their international showjumpers with great success.

Splints

This is the name given to a bony lump, which develops on the inside or outside of the front legs below the knee. The nearer they are to the knee, the more serious they are considered to be. In the United Kingdom years ago, splints were only seen on young horses that had been worked too hard, too young. Here they appear on horses of all ages, often while they are still unbroken in the paddock. Now they are being born with them if the paddock is sick enough!

The reason for this is (predictably) inadequate bone-building material in the feed when the horse was growing, similar to the cause of open knees. In the long-term, amend the diet so that the horse receives the correct supplements for the rest of its life. Quite often, a few weeks on the correct minerals with good remineralised pasture and balanced feed is enough to ensure the splints will disappear of their own accord.

One of my clients with a very good endurance horse regularly gives it a rest each year in a shockingly unhealthy paddock. The splints come up within four days of its being out, and disappear in the same time when he brings it back into work. I have pointed out that this is *not* the ideal scenario!

Treat the splint with a compress of comfrey leaves mashed or heated slightly and applied to the area under a bandage; emu oil is another useful option. This often helps clear the swellings up after two or three days, unless they are very deep-seated, in which case it may take a little longer.

The old method was to rub in castor oil two or three times a week over a period of a few weeks or paint on iodine twice a week. Both these methods produced a blister, which originally was considered the only cure. The methods suggested above are preferable and do work.

Sprains

These can occur in any joint, muscle or ligament at any time. But they are far more likely to happen in horses that have not and are not being fed a proper bone-building ration. If the bones do not develop properly the attachments for the tendons and ligaments will be insufficient.

Bandage the affected part with a pad soaked in cider vinegar (neat or fifty per cent in water) and some liquid from boiled comfrey leaves as well if it is available. The patient must not be ridden, but should be kept quiet in a small yard where it cannot move around too much, until the signs of the sprain have disappeared. If it is on a high feed, a bran mash should be given and the food cut down *immediately*. Otherwise turn the horse out for a month or two on a good paddock with a few feeds a week (for the minerals). This is usually all that is needed to rest the affected joint or tendon. It is a waste of time to turn it out in a paddock that has not been analysed and remineralised.

A rider I know, having got his horse's bones and teeth to their correct hardness (horse dentists do not appreciate very hard teeth as a rule!), decided to see how long it would take to revert to an unhealthy state if he stopped all supplementation. It took six weeks for the teeth (and therefore the bones) to be quite chalky again.

There is a homeopathic combination that works extremely well for these conditions: Ruta graveolens and arnica. I use these liquids with remarkable effect (on myself). They have also helped with horses. 200 c is the arnica strength I recommend, with 30 c of the Ruta graveolens. Give each substance in turn, three hours apart, for two days, then twice a day and then down to once. Try to keep the patient from exercising too much.

Stifle, slipping and/or locking

This condition is also caused by horses not getting their proper minerals. Over the last fifteen years or so, my hack has usually been a loan from someone who has had a problem with it. Nearly every horse slips its stifle when it comes.

This mostly occurs in horses that are wandering along and are not up to the bit at a walk or uncoordinated trot. All the horses I have looked after did this far too frequently when they first came, but after a couple of months on the right feed it did not happen any more. Again it appears to be environmental and depends on the health of the bones, tendons and ligaments. The old protocol used to be to get them fat so it would hold the joint in; others said do the reverse, but none of these methods worked. My solution seems to be more satisfactory!

Strangles

This is a bit like the chickenpox children contract; most young horses catch strangles at some stage or other and are usually immune to it from then on. In properly cared for horses, the condition does not progress further than a slightly swollen throat and runny nose, and runs a very short course with proper care. But if the horse is not healthy, strangles can be very serious indeed. It is intensely infectious in horses that are below par or not receiving their correct supplements.

Give 20 ml of vitamin C by injection daily and two table-spoons in the feed until the condition clears up. Usually one injection is all that is needed. Strangles vaccine seems unnecessary when the illness is caused by a basic lack of lime minerals and good feed. Respiratory problems are to be expected when there is a lack of calcium and magnesium.

One of the advantages of not vaccinating is that the horse will, if treated as above, build up its own antibodies.

Stringhalt

One of my old veterinary books states that stringhalt can happen to the forelegs as well, but I hope I never see it. This is a condition that affects one or both back legs, which are drawn up suddenly after each step at a walk. Curiously enough, even with quite severe stringhalt, horses seem to be able to gallop unimpeded. I know of several racehorses in the United Kingdom that suffered mildly from the condition in both back legs yet raced well nonetheless.

I have seen and heard of several horses in the last few years who only contracted stringhalt in one back leg, often pulling the leg up well above the belly at each step — a most uncomfortable-looking occurrence.

The most important response is to have one's paddock analysed and immediately top-dressed with lime minerals, whatever the time of year. Naturally occurring magnesium is the best cure. The master farrier and horse master Ron King told me that stringhalt often cleared up after the horse was taken off an offending paddock.

The first horse I treated with stringhalt had had it for two years, and it was six months before it was better. Severe cases are a problem, especially in heavy horses, because if they get down, their back legs do not work well enough for them to get up again. There is also a fashion to refer to stringhalt by different nationalities. I would suggest it is all just plain stringhalt!

Stringhalt is caused by a second-hand magnesium deficiency. The muscle enzymes are no longer working (see the section on magnesium) because there is not enough of the mineral available to the horse. Just giving dolomite and the correct supplements has cured a few horses after a time, but the quick cures did not happen until I realised that we had to find a special kind of magnesium. One of my clients in New South Wales was told to try magnesium orotate (orotates are minerals bonded with orotic acid or vitamin B13, which was discovered by Dr Robert Buist) and it clicked.

An affected horse needs all its correct supplements with an extra half teaspoon of borax twice a week and at least 4000 mg (8000 for a big horse) of magnesium orotate crushed up a day. The tablets come in 400 mcg; grind up the appropriate number and give them daily until the horse improves; this usually takes four to six days.

Improvement will *not* take place without exercise; the horse cannot go backwards and it cannot trot, but it can walk and do cantering work.

An event rider rang me a week or so before a major international event, and both her horses had stringhalt. I asked her which had the best chance and told her she should concentrate on riding it, giving them both the correct supplements meanwhile. The fancied horse won the event, the one left in the paddock was no worse, but no better either until she could give it the work that would help dissipate the magnesium round the muscles.

It is also very important to make sure the feed is as suggested in the last chapter, with no extra grains, just the bare minimum to keep the horse going, and only good pasture hay from a remineralised paddock. There is obviously a correlation with copper shortfall for this ailment because in a severe epidemic here five years ago, ninety-five per cent of cases rung in to me were blacks or chestnuts. Both have a high copper requirement when compared with other colours.

Stringhalt develops if a horse is turned out on capeweed or flat weed (both of which cause magnesium deficiency), and if it is fed on feed grown with superphosphate (which also inhibits magnesium). The only horses that have had to be shot with the complaint belonged to people who would not take this seriously and continued to feed them all food grown with chemical fertilisers. Sheree Roger's book, *Wellness Against All Odds*, gave me several pointers for dealing with this disease.

Tail eating

Whether this is an ailment or not, it is singularly annoying! A friend of mine who was making artificial tails noticed that ninety per cent of her orders all came from one area in Victoria — round Geelong. I did not know what was missing in the soils of that area, and nor did I find out until it became a popular place for alpaca farmers to set up their studs; when I saw the analyses from these farmers the problem was obvious. The soils there are incredibly low in everything that matters and have a pH to match.

Horses stop stripping each other's tails once they are receiving enough of the correct supplements. Tails, like wool, need a lot of minerals to grow. Keratin is needed for hair, and it in turn needs sulphur and copper.

Teething problems

A horse's teeth should be done at least twice yearly until it is six years old; after that they usually need doing at least once a year.

Any dribbling of the feed when eating, or undue chucking of the head when ridden, can mean the teeth need attention. A horse that pulls uncontrollably when ridden or cocks its jaw generally has teeth problems. The back teeth can become very ragged and sharp, causing considerable pain when the horse is eating or when it has a bit in its mouth.

Call in a horse dentist or someone who is qualified to check the teeth at once. A horse's feet and teeth should both be checked regularly.

I have heard of at least one racehorse that was condemned as a rogue and finally destroyed because of bad teeth. Too late, it was discovered that successive trainers had failed to notice that its teeth were causing it agony. At the yard where I worked in the United Kingdom, the first thing the head lad (foreman) did with a new arrival was to pull out its tongue, put in his hand and check that its teeth were in good order. Regrettably, on a great many occasions they were not, even when they came from quite good yards.

Occasionally, in young horses, wolf teeth need pulling if they are too crowded; this did not occur in young racehorses in the United Kingdom, so I suspect it is another of those problems due to inadequate bone-building minerals when young.

Older horses that have been put on the correct supplements will quite often show skeletal improvement within a couple of years. One old thoroughbred sprang its flat-sided ribs when fourteen years old and needed a new much longer girth. Bones and teeth will respond together.

> NOTE: Horses that have become injured due to improperly cared for teeth often respond well to a rubber bit. The pain gradually declines and eventually they can become quite easy to bit properly again. When I worked in racing, I usually got the bad pullers to ride, and had no problems (except with the foreman at first) when I rode them in a rubber bit.

Tetanus

Most horses are immunised for tetanus when young and boosted yearly. However, this is no guarantee that tetanus will not develop after a particular type of wound. Tetanus is caused by the bacillus clostridium tetanae, which flourishes in dirty, deep and airless puncture wounds. It is anaerobic in other words. A wound that bleeds freely is not usually at risk; in fact, tetanus often develops from a wound that has scarcely been noticed or seen.

There is some question these days about the efficacy of these immunisations. It is possible the organism has changed or mutated; this is what Bechamp, a contemporary of Louis Pasteur, said would happen with vaccines. The surroundings in which the bacteria live dictate their form. A different pH in the body will change the bacteria accordingly.

Bullet wounds may also become infected, particularly if caused by shotgun pellets. A tetanus immunisation does not mean that wounds may be left undisinfected and undressed; proper care should always be taken. This, sadly, does not always happen.

If there is concern after a deep wound (often in the foot), give a dessertspoon of vitamin C in the food twice a day, or 20 cc by injection daily for fourteen days at least after injury.

Tetanus usually develops in ten to twelve days, but has been known to take longer. Should tetanus be suspected, tap the horse smartly under the chin and the eyes will roll back. Eventually the jaw will also lock (lockjaw was the old name for the complaint).

In this case, give 50 ml of vitamin C intravenously if possible, otherwise it can be injected in the muscle. Repeat every two hours until the horse improves. Keep the patient quiet, as any sudden noise may send it into convulsions, which are a danger to itself and everyone else. A small dog that developed tetanus after a car accident took exactly twenty minutes to relax. I treated him the moment his jaw locked, as I had not been sure what was wrong.

It is no good instituting the vitamin C treatment two or three days after the tetanus has become established. Speed is essential, and you should give mega doses every two hours. One very cross lady who rang me four days after her horse developed tetanus was furious because it did not clear up at once.

With our present knowledge of the efficacy of vitamin C for this condition, there should be no reason for a horse to suffer this terrible illness. I have nursed a horse through it before we knew about vitamins. It was a traumatic experience.

Travel tetany

This is the name for a condition caused by a lack of magnesium, like all tetanies. Read the section on magnesium carefully and it will be seen that, even if magnesium was present in the first place, it can be lost very easily. Hot weather, in particular, causes it to be lost from the tissues. Any trembling (at any time, bar extreme cold, but possibly then too) means the horse has run out of magnesium. Treat it at once.

Tying up

Tying up seems to be a problem anywhere that horses are raced these days. Thirty or more years ago, it was virtually unknown. Therefore, again, it would appear to be caused by a deficiency of some kind. It comes back to ensuring the basic mineral supplementation is received. Horses that get all their minerals, seaweed meal ad lib and cider vinegar just do not suffer from the tying up syndrome. Like azoturia, it can also be due to excessive protein in the wrong place and at the wrong time. It does not seem to occur in a horse that has been properly fed its minerals from birth. The main deficiencies responsible appear to be magnesium, potassium, iodine, selenium and vitamin E; the last two work together. Remember if the horse is iodine deficient it will be unable to make use of other vitamins and minerals.

One mare I rode regularly often tied up when racing, but once the correct minerals were added to her diet she never did it again. Vitamin E was not necessary in her case, however, as mentioned in the section on that vitamin, many horses improve when they are receiving it.

Urinary and genital tract infections

Like vaginal tract infections, the cause of these is basically a lack of vitamin A. If the horse receives a tablespoon of cod-liver oil occasionally it should not occur. Give a vitamin A supplement of at least 80,000 units or their equivalent daily for the first week and a tablespoon of vitamin C in the feed daily. The trouble should clear up. If the horse is at grass, make sure that chemical fertilisers are not used on the paddocks and that they have been remineralised. Artificial fertilisers on their own could cause this condition, as they reduce vitamin A.

Genital tract infections should not occur in healthy mares. The cause is similar to urinary tract infections. Vitamin A is the most important factor in the health of the genital tract, and often a course of this vitamin will clear up quite stubborn cases. Extra vitamin C (as above) should also be given. Any mare that has had this complaint should be swabbed before going to the stallion, as occasionally an organism can be transmitted to the stallion (and from him to the next mare).

Drugs are not always the answer. Proper minerals in the feed and a healthy, remineralised paddock will usually clear up the condition.

Urinary calculi

A vet should be consulted immediately if this is suspected, as it is very painful. The horse will stand as though trying to urinate, but with little if any result. Mares do not as a rule suffer from this ailment, as their ureters are shorter and wider than those of a male. Regular cider vinegar in the horse's diet will break down the calculi eventually and ensure that it does not recur.

Urinary calculi can be caused by an imbalance in the feed, or by very mineralised bore water. Prevention is definitely better than cure, as with many other conditions.

It is always worth trying some crushed magnesium orotate tablets for four or five days; six of the 400 mg tablets daily on the food should help. An excess of calcium (from lucerne or whatever) can also be a contributory cause.

Uveitis

This is a complaint which eventually ends up with the patient having to have an eye removed.

However, when a change in the diet occurs — including remineralising the paddock — it clears up completely in every case. One of my hacks was a black-skinned, strawberry-marked Apaloosa minus one eye; its problems were all linked to ongoing copper deficiencies and I suspect the reason for it losing its eye was the same.

Vaccinations, see section on immunisation reactions

Warts

Another magnesium (and vitamin C) deficiency condition. As a horse makes its own supply of the latter, add dolomite to the ration and the wart(s) will drop off in about a week or less.

White line disease (onychomycosis), previously known as canker

This disease is causing havoc across the United States and the United Kingdom, and has been observed since 1980. It is nothing worse than a very advanced case of seedy toe, or possibly another, similar organism. It does not arise unless copper is too low or lacking in the horse's system.

The pictures I have seen of this condition are quite horrific. Whole feet ulcerate away, and there are many horses in the world racing on Equilox (this is a plastic material used to make an artificial foot, in effect, and is very costly).

The farrier who brought this to my attention has worked in Kentucky bluegrass country and I know from my English and Irish clients that the same thing is happening there too. NPK and nitrogenous fertilisers (often in the form of DAP — di-ammonium phosphate) are now being used extensively on what was arguably the best grass-growing country in the United States, United Kingdom and Ireland. All these types of fertilisers completely suppress copper; this fact was hammered home by Andre Voisin and Lady Eve Balfour in the 1950s. The disease has been reported in Australia also. Copper washes to curb the putrefaction and proper feeding are the answer.

Horrific pictures of a chestnut, Welsh cob stallion's feet were sent to me; he was apparently still serving his mares, but had been moving around on what looked like great lumps of rotten flesh. Every drug had been tried, yeast infections had been suspected (why?), but nothing had worked. It was an uphill battle to convince the owners to change his diet completely, and to include copper sulphate and seaweed. The last photos sent to me were of the farrier trimming up four normal-looking feet!

Windsucking (crib biting)

Prevention and correct feeding is the only answer to this condition. Keeping a strap round the horse's neck to stop it sucking wind, which otherwise fills its stomach, has been the usual protocol. This practice acts to decrease the appetite. Horses with a stomach full of wind do not feel hungry, which is why those that consistently windsuck become unthrifty.

When visiting a stud in New South Wales a few years ago, the owner told me that she had just run out of copper sulphate the previous day. By the next morning four out of about ten of the visiting mares had started windsucking. I asked her to let me know how soon after the reintroduction of copper in the diet they stopped. It took three or four hours. I had always believed that this habit, once contracted, stayed for life — this is not so, apparently.

Wobblers

This is another of those strangely named diseases which I have never seen; I have advised the owners of these animals to start feeding them correctly and it has cleared up. Possibly it is another magnesium deficiency state, as the name implies. It bears a very faint resemblance to mild stringhalt, I gather. The health of the paddocks should definitely be considered and a full remineralisation program implemented.

Worms

An alternative strategy for worms
For the last thirty-five years I have not used a proprietary drench on any animal, horses and brood mares included. When I feel they need worming, I raise the copper sulphate levels in their feed accordingly. If you are in any doubt, have a vet do a worm count.

In the old days, one knew when animals were wormy; they were ill-tempered, their eyes tended to be runny and they were picky with their feed. Using the correct amounts of copper suggested in the feed has been tried on other animals with equal success.

I was encouraged to try this for several reasons. One was a fear of the toxic after-effects of many of the conventional drenches which seemed, apparently, to be the only answer; the other was the knowledge that horse masters of old used copper, although there was no mention of the amounts given.

The most compelling reason for trying this method can be found in the collected works of one of the world's greatest soil scientists, Dr W A Albrecht. He proved that animals whose systems contained the correct amount of copper did not suffer from interior parasites. The animals could eat worm eggs in the paddock, but the worms did not stay in the animal once they hatched if the copper intake was correct.

A teaspoon (4–5 g) of copper sulphate per day, per horse, is a good base to start from.

Research done in Japan on humans, which showed that black-haired people required at least double the amount of copper that fair-haired ones did, points to why horses' doses might need to vary.

We now know that all horses need about 5 g per day. Black-coloured horses and the cancer-prone colours, grey and chestnut, patently need that amount plus more in many cases.

A school child's microscope can be used to monitor the presence of worms. In New Zealand, most farmers do their own counts for all stock. If a worm count is taken and it is 150 eggs per gram or below, it is quite satisfactory.

A friend has a thirty-two year old buckskin gelding that she looks after at an animal aid place near Sydney. He had a worm count of around 3000 when she first got him, and no known drench had any effect at all. They had all been tried and he did not look too good. We started him on high levels of copper (with his other minerals) and he began to look better and better. We settled on two tablespoons a day, and he now looks marvellous. The worms are decreasing steadily, and have come down to 800. He is only getting one tablespoon now. Everyone remarks on how well he looks, so the parameters are fairly wide.

This experience is borne out by the University of Minnesota's research on ponies and copper intake. They tried to kill the first ones they started with, but failed to do so. At the end of the experiment they were still receiving amounts that would stop most other animals in their tracks, and were extremely well. They were not getting dolomite either; this can act as a brake on copper toxicity without stopping its usefulness.

In the United Kingdom in the middle of the 1950s, one of the French steeplechasers, a consistent winner, regularly passed the largest roundworms I have ever seen. They were as thick as a rope, and more than a metre long. Cleaning out his box in the morning could be a daunting task. No one even remarked on the phenomenon and he was never medicated!

Modern anthelmintic drenches

Drenches are only a short-term answer to the worm problem; good nutrition, healthy pastures and good farm practice are the long-term solution. Worms were not the problem they are now in days gone by and I do not remember actual worming. Chemical farming, however, has decreased the ability of the natural fauna of the paddocks to process the manure. Also, the horse's natural resistance to interior parasites has been lowered due to the lack of copper in their feed. Copper is also totally inhibited by artificial manures of the phosphatic or nitrogenous variety.

Another rather chilling factor emerged a few years ago. Many people find it difficult to believe that the six week drench is no longer necessary when they are feeding their horses correctly, so they still continue the practice. In no case was a worm count taken *before* this procedure, which surely would have been common sense and would probably have saved the worming taking place.

There have been two deaths and one near death (they rang me in time) after drenching with the usual drench, whatever it was. Some of the horses had been receiving their copper supplementation and some had not. I do not know what brand of drenches were involved, but the people concerned used them with their vet's blessing. It took their horses four days to die. All the vet could say apologetically was, 'It happens sometimes'. That was my comment about one top showjumper; 'It takes a long time to get them up there'. The question is did they die of anaphylactic shock, the cumulative effects of the drench, or were they in some way unstable? The one horse I treated in time was saved with fairly large amounts of vitamin C given in a hurry.

I was told in the 1960s by the vets at the University of Melbourne that you could not rid a paddock of worms, no matter how long you rested it. But I think that if worms never reach maturity, they will eventually give up. Copper does not kill them; worms merely will not stay in an animal whose copper reserves are correct. Part of their life-cycle needs to be spent inside an animal.

Of all the worms to which horses are prone, the red worms that are blood suckers are possibly the worst. They certainly cause the most havoc in improperly fed horses, especially young ones. Red worm does not just confine itself to the intestines, it goes right through the whole body. I was given a trotting cross mare when she was six months old. Her red worm infestation was so bad that she passed nothing else for a week and suffered long-term brain damage. I taught the children to ride on her, but her scattiness had to be watched.

Foals should be on the correct copper ration from birth, sharing their dam's feed until they get their own. Their appetite is smaller, so they consume the right amount. Try the methods suggested above, which are in any case only part of a healthy feeding regime.

9 General feeding and care of stud horses

The necessity for healthy fodder has been emphasised right through this book; the preceding chapter on ailments merely highlights this. Most, if not all, of the illnesses that affect horses would not occur if they and their dams had been fed properly from the time of their conception. Food in this instance includes the pasture on their paddocks. Mares and stallions that are malnourished and deficient in the necessary minerals cannot breed tough, healthy foals.

It is most important that stud owners attend to the state of their land and see that the mineral balance is as good as possible. In the last few years, I have advised in cases where foals have been born with bone deformities like splints; in every case the mares had been on really sick paddocks coming up to foaling, and were apparently unfed and unsupplemented. It is a strange idea that animals do not need good food until they are actually lactating: I first encountered this attitude in the dairy industry and found it hard to take.

Handfeeding the necessary minerals and vitamins in the bucket is effective to some extent. However, there is absolutely no doubt that the feed is assimilated better when it does not have to offset sickly and badly-grown pasture as well. After all, a horse eats roughly ninety to ninety five per cent of its feed off the paddock. It therefore *must* be analysed and brought into balance.

It is not an accident that some of our best bloodstock is reared in the Hunter Valley in New South Wales; the soil there appears to be very good, although the amounts of conventional fertilisers being used on some studs are beginning to cause trouble.

Similarly, horses bred and reared in New Zealand, where the soil, unlike Australia, is generally high in calcium and magnesium are, as long as they only come over from New Zealand for short periods, usually tougher and sounder than many of their Australian counterparts.

When one considers the nutritional handicaps suffered by most horses reared in Australia, and their often excellent performances when up against horses from other countries, it is obvious that we are breeding genetically very good stock indeed. It is a pity to waste that potential by not rearing them properly.

After a drought

One fact must be remembered and that is that the grass that comes away after drought or a long dry does not deliver its minerals (always assuming that they are there) for at least six weeks. Dr George Miller, a vet in the Gippsland Department of Agriculture, worked that one out, and it makes sense. I always noticed that stock of all kinds seemed to get ill after that first autumn 'break', or the first green after a long drought.

Hay

Hay will have to be fed through winter in most areas. The most important fact any feeder of livestock should remember is that animals can tolerate very cold weather as long as they are not hungry. Keeping warm requires extra feed and, if there is a sudden cold spell, the ration must be increased for its duration. Extra hay (if it is good) will cover this.

The absolute, and not unattainable ideal is for every stud to remineralise a paddock or two each year (if they cannot do the whole stud), and then make sure they grow their own hay on those paddocks.

Hand-feeding stud horses and mares

All stud horses should be getting a hard ration as well as their grazing. The amount given each day will depend entirely on the grazing available, its quality and the time of year. In spring, if the paddocks are healthy and remineralised, one small (around the kilogram mark) feed daily is often enough for the first few months; see chapter seven on amounts. The moment the grass starts to die back in the drier areas, or decreases in quality, as happens in the more temperate parts of Australia like Gippsland, the feeds will have to be raised to two a day. These feeds will need to be at least three-quarters chaff and bran, with the remaining quarter grain. They must contain all the supplementary minerals.

Again, refer to chapter seven for feeding practice. This method works just as well for breeding horses. The type of grain depends on the preference of the stud breeder. I prefer soaked barley for the reasons below, with a little sunflower and maize as an extra if the weather turns very cold.

Barley has a great advantage in that it contains natural vitamin B5 which is needed for the horse's *own* production of cortisone. The advantage of soaking one of the grains is that the liquid used can incorporate some of the water-soluble minerals that may be needed and the cider vinegar. It then serves to dampen the feed, which has to be done in any case. It is impossible nowadays to give horses dry feed; the dust factor is too high, and lung troubles can be caused by it.

Providing the stud's own (remineralised) hay

If the owner of a stud is fortunate enough to be able to grow all the hay and grain that is needed organically and on remineralised paddocks, the health of the horses will benefit immensely. Unfortunately this will be the exception; most studs have to make do with chemically-grown fodder they buy in. The artificial fertilisers will have, as usual, inhibited the uptake of calcium, magnesium, copper, sulphur and therefore selenium, and other trace minerals as well as some of the vitamins.

It will be necessary to add the following minerals and vitamins to the feed of all breeding horses whether mares or stallions:

A tablespoon of dolomite per feed;

A tablespoon of milling sulphur per day;

Seaweed on demand — make a two-sectioned box on the cross-member of the stable/shed and put seaweed meal in one half and rock salt in the other;

100 ml of cider vinegar daily. This is particularly important for stallions at all times and mares in the last

months of pregnancy as it ensures easy births. (Personally, I prefer to feed it permanently, as it also helps prevent stones in the kidney and elsewhere.)

A tablespoon of cod-liver oil once a week.

If foals are born to mares deficient in these vitamins, they may be born with contracted tendons, or be so short of vitamin A that they will not live very long (nine days is the longest they can survive without the vitamin).

The directions in chapter seven on soaking grain — preferably barley — and adding cider vinegar and copper should be followed. This mixture should be used to dampen the feed.

On deficient land that has not been top-dressed, all of the above will have to be fed without fail on a daily basis. For land that has been analysed and top-dressed, it will take at least a year (more if there is a bad drought) before the missing minerals reach the grass. Then, and only then, following a second satisfactory analysis, the feeds may be cut to three times a week. As long as hard feed is fed, it will be necessary to feed the rest of the supplements suggested above. As mentioned, the fodder will almost certainly have been grown with artificial phosphorus or nitrogen in some form or another, ensuring that the feed will be almost totally deficient in copper and many other minerals.

Ponies

Ponies and crossbred horses will need a fraction of the amounts needed by thoroughbreds. Both may do very well on two or three feeds per week, or one small one daily. They obviously do not have the same requirement as thoroughbreds, but they too suffer from founder and allied calcium/magnesium and copper-deficiency conditions. They will still need supplementary dolomite and sulphur (a dessertspoon of each daily). They will also definitely need their 3 g of copper daily at least (or 5 g if they are big-bodied) and more if copper-deficiency conditions arise. All horses, whatever their sex, will need seaweed meal on a self-help basis, no matter how good the grazing is.

'Dry' pregnant mares

These should receive the same amount of minerals as lactating ones, and just slightly less feed for the first few months of pregnancy, unless they are being worked and then they will be fed as normal. Empty mares must have all their minerals or they will stay that way. Copper deficiency prevents them from cycling normally and a lack of vitamin A (cod-liver oil) stops them holding to service!

Stallions

It is particularly important that all of the above is implemented with stallions. If they are not fed correctly, their fertility will be affected. This is often the result of a mineral and vitamin-deficient diet (particularly vitamins A and D) and will be irreversible in the male.

Poison sprays

Do not use sprays near your breeding animals. Many years ago, when there were birth deformities in children in central Gippsland, it was supposed that mothers had been exposed to dioxin sprays, which were used quite heavily in those days. Our landlord bought a stallion from that area that traced straight back to one of the greats of the past — St Simon — and we all looked forward to his first crop. The mares were all classically-bred Arabs and thoroughbred stock mares, all very fit, healthy and good foal producers. Bill rang me up when the first foal arrived to the best of the Arabian mares, 'Come and have a look, it's wrong and I do not understand it.' I went up to their farm and they had the foal in a barn. As it lay there, the horrid truth dawned — its head was the size of a full-grown horse. There were ten mares that were to foal, and only two achieved healthy foals. In the others the deformities ranged from eyeless sockets to foals similar to the first, and many other aberrations. It was not the females who had caused their offspring's deformities, but the stallion.

It took three years before the poison was out of the stallion's system. The next year there were a couple of wrong foals, but after that they were fine. See that your breeding stock *never* has contact with poison sprays of any kind. There really is not a safe substance around.

Weeds

Sprays are not and never have been the answer to this so-called problem. Weeds only show up an imbalance in the soil; getting the land back in line mineralwise will go a long way to clearing up the trouble. In any case the more species there are in a pasture, the healthier the animals. Ryegrass and fesque or any other type of monoculture grasses are totally unhealthy. Newman Turner looked for a minimum of forty-five and preferred sixty-five mixed species in his paddocks in the 1950s.

Sulphur

It is particularly important that stallions are given the diet above. Sulphur is essential and, without the amino acids cysteine and methionine in the gut, selenium is not available. Sperm require selenium to stay healthy; if it is missing, their flagellum (tails) drop off, they become weak and are not able to reach their destination.

Seaweed is equally important to have freely available; it contains selenium and zinc as well as all the other trace minerals and iodine in natural form. The prostate gland has the highest concentration of zinc of any gland in the body. If this is not supplied in the diet, problems will follow. Both these minerals are amply supplied in seaweed. The weekly allowance of cod-liver oil (vitamins A and D) is also very important; 20 ml of cod-liver oil in the feed once a week is all that is needed. Should a stallion become deficient in vitamin A, permanent sterility can result (see above).

Water

If stallions are confined to hard bore water, they must be given their ration of cider vinegar daily, which will prevent urinary calculi, a fatal condition in male animals. It is also important that the water supply be from a good bore or rainwater, not fluorided. These days it is wise to always check water quality.

Weaners

These will need a nourishing diet including about half of the minerals suggested above. Good grazing is particularly important, but unfortunately at weaning time the grazing is often poor due to the time of year. Plenty of good plain hay that is well grown should be given. Grass and clover hay is all right, as long as it is no more than half clover; refer again to chapter three and make sure that the weaner's pastures are free of artificial pasture boosters and have been tested and remineralised. One small hard feed a day will be necessary. It should be:

>   One part lucerne chaff;
>   One part oaten chaff;
>   One part bran; and

Half a part grain — barley is preferred.
Mix the above with the usual supplements and ensure seaweed and rock salt are freely available in a shelter or covered
feeder.

10 Conditioning of working horses and recuperation after injury

I will start this section by referring to an excellent paper that appeared in *Horse and Rider* by Deborah Lucas in November 1989. It is entitled, 'Fit not fat, the dangers of overfeeding your horse'. Lucas's article underlines my point that there should be some rib definition in performance horses. When a client says they can see its ribs, I tell them not to worry.

She also points out that this regimen *starts* before birth; over-fat foals in utero and on the ground will not make good strong horses with hard bone; she points out that such foals have 'post' feet, and the pastern is almost without definition.

Conditioning

This chapter is written for those who have read the rest of the book and have their horses on the nutritional program suggested. It is useless to implement a conditioning program if a horse is not being properly fed — they will not stand up to continued hard work, nor will their legs and sinews stay sound.

Please remember that ninety-five per cent (at least) of the food taken in by any horse comes from its paddock. Therefore it is of the utmost importance that the soil has been tested and remineralised, and is not subjected to artificial manures.

Pre-training for any discipline

When I wrote the first edition of this book in 1989, I assumed (wrongly) that a discussion of conditioning horses would not be necessary. Racehorses in Australia and the United States usually go through a period of pre-training these days — often done by an outside contractor. Modern English trainers also have their charges pre-trained for six weeks before they bring them into solid work, walking and trotting, whether they are freshly broken or coming in from a spell. Prior to the 1960s, the pre-training went on with the normal training. We were sent out for one to two hours road work, walking and trotting, generally not seeing the gallops at all for the first month. This process ensures that the muscles and tendons of the legs and body are as fit as they can be before the fast work begins and applies equally to all disciplines.

There are large numbers of horses out there doing dressage, showjumping, western work, showing, endurance or being used as hacks, who need conditioning as well as their appointed work. Endurance riders, hunters and three-day event competitors usually know more about hardening their horses up — they have to. Often the other categories are owned by people who feel that their horses do not need as much preparation for the demands of their discipline.

Warming up before work

All of us would be familiar with seeing athletes warming up before their competitions and walking or jogging. Seeing horses treated in the same manner is not so usual, but it should be as there's a lot more horse!

I have seen dressage horses and racehorses come out of their stables or yards, and saddled up before going straight into deep sand or a similar arena, or a small 400 metre track to do their 'work out' and then go straight back to their stables afterwards with no warming up or cooling down, which is often all the exercise their owners have time to give them. Cutting and western horses often go through a similar regime.

Inevitably over a period of time, often quite short, a host of leg problems from navicular disease to windgalls begin to appear and the legs show every signs of imminent collapse. I receive a number of calls from people with quite young western horses suffering from navicular disease and other leg troubles, for the same reason. The demands on their legs for camp drafting, cutting, reining and western training are quite considerable. Fortunately many of the latter actually work cattle as part of their daily routine and so ensure they are reasonably hardened.

Signs of leg problems

Windgalls are soft swellings that appear round and above the pasterns. They are not serious in themselves, but they are a warning that the legs and joints are being strained without being hardened first. Heat in any part of the leg or joints should receive full attention.

I suggest that these horses be given *at least twenty minutes* road work prior to starting work each time they are ridden. If they are only worked once a week, at least two other evenings must be allotted to it as well. The excuses are usually legion (and some quite valid) as to why this is impossible. I know the roads in most districts are not safe for horses, and that many people do not have the time for roadwork, but as I have pointed out, the soundness of their horses depends on it. The reason that doing roadwork is 'too dull' I will pass over. What they are doing is like expecting a normal person to start advanced athletics without the strengthening exercises needed initially.

Most horse owners have a float, or access to one, and there are good tracks in the hills or minor unsealed roads within reach of nearly all big towns. In the summer a rock-hard paddock would do the job fairly well, but might, if it was the horse's own paddock, lead to boredom. We were taught never to work a horse in its own paddock for this reason. The racehorse trainer I rode for near Melbourne would take his horses up into the hills of west Gippsland when they were in full work at least once a week. We would work them up the mountain tracks at a reasonable speed, keeping them nicely balanced and his horses did not suffer either from the leg troubles or the boredom that continual track work often induces. Even dressage, show or western horses need a change of scene, and to stretch their legs occasionally — for their mental processes as much as anything else.

Conditioning horses and riders

Conditioning hunters in the United Kingdom for a long hunting season involved four hours road work a day for a couple of months. This was very expensive in shoes! All riders must make the effort to give their horses strengthening work before expecting them to do anything else if they wish them to stay sound in wind and limb. Another aspect of this regime, which is not always considered, is that the riders will *also* need to be hard and fit. This is very important, so paying someone else to condition your horse is not always a good idea! It is not fair on a really fit horse to be piloted by a rider who is *not*! After a spate of particularly awful accidents in three-day events in the United Kingdom, one of the senior riders suggested that these days, neither riders nor their horses receive the toughening up in the hunting field that they used to get when eventing started. I went to the first Badminton three-day event and although the jumps looked terrifying to tackle in cold blood they were actually no worse than those we consistently meet when out hunting.

Three stages of getting a horse fit

When getting a horse fit for racing, eventing or showjumping from scratch, there are three almost distinct stages. The first one is when they come in off grass or are uneducated. This used to be known as the green stage. At this time, they need to be ridden up to the bit, and made to think about what they are doing.

The second stage comes after a period of up to two months when they start to feel well and enjoy their work. Often the feed is slightly increased at this stage. I used to call it the stupid time because it was when people got tipped off or the horses banged themselves. They are just feeling their oats, to use an old expression!

The third and final stage when a horse is fully fit is when they settle down to their work. Then there are little if any high jinks; they feel good and just get on with the job at hand. All this is assuming they are being given the right amount of exercise at all stages to occupy them both mentally and physically. It is particularly important not to allow boredom to creep in — for horse or rider.

I watched a camp draughter repeat the same manoeuvre with her horse for about three-quarters of an hour — after which it bucked her off. She was lucky it waited so long!

Interval training

This was very fashionable in the middle of the 1990s, and has been the downfall of several horse owners. I read an article by a leading international three-day event rider in an English magazine; he said that, 'interval training in the hands of idiots was very dangerous.' I would not put it quite so bluntly but, judging by the phone calls I've received, there have been many problems. Each client said that their horses looked marvellous and were 'really big and strong', but because interval training happened very quickly the legs had not been strengthened to carry the extra weight, and the horse was in bad trouble as a result. Interval training can produce this effect in quite a short time. These horses (as emphasised above) *must* spend at least the same amount of time on steady roadwork as they do on their interval training.

Children's ponies

Children on horses and ponies who canter them along the roads have animals which seemingly never suffer from leg problems, unlike those that are sedately exercised on the lunge prior to work by their careful owners. These owners would probably be better on top of the horses (as suggested by that very experienced horseman Henry Wynmalen many years ago) exercising them on the roads, not necessarily flat out, but a collected trot and an extended walk would do very well. Remember, far more horses are broken down on soft rather than hard surfaces.

Alois Podharsky

I would recommend a book that I read about fifteen years ago to *all* horse owners. It is *My Horses, My Teachers* by Alois Podhajsky, who was one of the top dressage and high school riders of the world. His views on making a horse go forward willingly and the means he used to do so — lots of long rides in the country, jumping and hunting — are fascinating to read. He took on all types and breeds of horses, including many that had been branded as hopeless, and turned them into beautiful rides and top dressage horses as well. This book seems to be available again worldwide; see the Bibliography for details.

Recuperation after injury

This also includes bringing horses back into work. I decided to add this section to this edition of *Natural Horse Care* because of the many enquiries on the subject from people who seemed to have no experience in this field.

All of us at some time or other have to bring a horse back into active work after injury or illness, and there is a difference.

Stringhalt, for example, is *not* an injury, and well-meaning advice to 'shut the animal up' is definitely counter-productive.

Those who have read this far (see the section on stringhalt in chapter eight) will know that *stringhalt* is a product of severe secondhand magnesium deficiency, not unlike founder. In both cases, the remedy has to be used with quiet continuous exercise to produce a quick result. Without it the horse becomes no worse, but nor does it recover.

Motor damage

Strained tendons, ligaments and, very occasionally, cracked bones are all definitely motor injuries. They were far rarer in Europe in the days when I worked with performance horses than they are now. I think this was because the land was so much healthier, horses got their bone-building minerals in their normal feed. Thus the 'projections' that supported the tendons and ligaments were well-formed and did their job. I never saw a young horse with open knees (or heard of it). Young stock developed good, flat bone with plenty of definition.

I remember a stud master in Australia asking me to look at a new arrival, as it had 'funny knees'. They had flat, strong bone plates and were beautifully formed. He had seen his first horse with really strong knees! See the section on epiphysitis.

Young stock must be fed as outlined in the previous chapter and then we have something to work on should bone, tendon or ligament injury arise.

People ring to consult me about one or any of these injuries and we work out a food regime. Sometimes the affected part also needs strapping, and massage and support can also be quite helpful. Then they want to fill it with painkillers — arnica if they follow me or butazolidin if they do not. Pain is there for a reason, however. The senior teaching vet at Melbourne University taught me in the early 1960s the disadvantages of masking pain; the animals behaved as though they had no injury at all, which was terrible to see. If the pain is such that the horse does not want to eat, small amounts of arnica are in order, otherwise nothing should be administered.

The patient needs to be let right down. Put it on a mild non-heating ration with *no* grain. Losing a little weight will not hurt either. A racehorse trainer, who was also a vet, in Sussex, England between the wars, ran what were always known as 'Jerry Langford's breakdowns'. They were skin, muscle and bone, shining and fit, and carried no unnecessary weight at all. They won races, and although all had fairly serious injuries, Jerry got them sound and kept them that way by *not* overfeeding them and allowing them to get too big.

An injured horse should be confined in a small yard or paddock, so there is no incentive for it to move around too much. Its new diet should keep it pretty placid, and thus the injured limb will be exercised and not lose muscle tone. This is very important.

As it becomes sounder and the lameness is not visible, a little mild exercise on even ground, led by its keeper, can be started. At this juncture, the owner usually asks if it can be lunged. I would not recommend this, as lunging is strictly for the experts and horses that are sound in all four legs. It can put an intolerable strain on a newly-healed injury. Gradually, the horse can be brought back into quiet work, and the hardening up process will start all over again!

Case histories

In the early 1960s, a nice young (unbroken) thoroughbred gelding was crushed against a gate in horseplay — literally. Its shoulder was badly cracked and the owners were going to shoot it. I asked them to let me have it for a few weeks. I confined it in a run of about 15 m square and got it used to being handled quietly (their efforts in 'breaking' were rather old-fashioned). There was not much I could do for it except give it the right food, and massage the shoulder occasionally with comfrey oil. In exactly four weeks, almost to the day, its shoulder had knit together, and it went on to be a very useful stock horse.

Another case which worked against all conventional wisdom was when I treated a hunter who had a total breakdown in the 1950s. The tendon had gone and the near fore was resting on the ground. He was a big, strong horse and injury arose because he had struck into himself when landing into holding clay from a drop jump. The front legs could not clear and the cut looked fairly superficial. The local vet suggested I bandage it and take him out again once the cut had healed, as he did not consider it had bruised the tendon sheath. We were both wrong — no scans were available then — and total breakdown was the result.

The vet told me to turn him out on the best land I could find — Cranbourne Chase in Dorset, in that case — for eighteen months. I did, by which time I was working in racing. I fetched him, absolutely sound, and sold him to a huntsman who rode him for another fifteen years. Rest is a great healer, but few people have the facilities, time or inclination!

Needless to say, horses with totally broken bones or compound fractures are very unlikely to recover. I have healed a few young horses with careful splinting and bandaging, but a large horse is too heavy for the weight to be taken by its legs. Euthanasing the horse quickly and quietly is the best option.

11 Blood analysis

For performance horses, blood analysis is a valuable diagnostic aid which has been developed over the last few years. In the past, horses raced without the trainer having much idea of the animal's blood picture. Trainers were obliged to depend on their knowledge and judgement to know whether a horse was fully fit or not. We learnt how to gauge this reasonably successfully.

However, blood analysis will be a waste of time and money if the horse's mineral and vitamin requirements have not been fully met in its diet. It is important that the horses are fed as I have suggested in this book and hopefully their mineral and vitamin needs will then be satisfied. The analysis should tell the trainer if the nutrients have been properly utilised and enable any shortfalls to be met.

The vet in charge of the blood testing will explain fully the meaning of the various terms in the blood analysis. So I will only give a brief breakdown of the various tests here to enable a horse owner to have some idea of the processes involved.

The bilirubin test (often just referred to as 'bili')

The test should always be well within the preferred range (a normal part of any blood test). If the liver is not performing correctly, measures must be taken immediately to find out why and remedy the situation.

Even before the blood is consulted, the liver function test is possibly the most important one of the lot. The average in any animal is around seven; anything much above or much lower is grounds for great concern. I saw a herd of Holstein Friesian milking cattle in the United Kingdom who all showed a level of 0.05. They were trying to die.

Fortunately, the liver recovers more easily than almost any other organ (read the section on vitamin B15 in chapter five). The cow's malaise was due to a supplement containing minerals that had all been chelated; this is very dangerous by mouth. All recovered when fed the same minerals in basic form.

So make sure when you have blood analysis done that the bilirubin test *is* included, and consult it first — the liver has to be in good order.

Composition of blood

Blood is made up of approximately forty per cent corpuscles and sixty per cent plasma. The plasma carries the protein, enzymes and electrolytes. The corpuscles (cells) are divided into three categories: red, white and platelets. Red blood cells contain haemoglobin, which carries oxygen, and is itself dependent on the iron (and therefore copper) intake of the horse for its health (see chapter four, iron *cannot* be assimilated without copper). White blood cells (leucocytes) are responsible for the health of the body — they control stresses caused by infections, immune reactions, injuries and allergies. This is the reason why, in nearly every case of a horse being below par, the number of white blood cells in the blood will often dramatically increase. Should this phenomenon turn up in an apparently healthy horse, trouble could be around the corner. The white blood cells are the first defence against disease. They are multiplying to enable them to destroy the pathogenic organisms that are about to attack. Modern blood tests come into their own at this point. They can tell the horse owner and vet the nature of the invading organism. Then sensitivity tests can be done and the appropriate drug used.

> *NOTE: Quite often mega-doses of vitamin C will work wonders; injections and oral administration should occur together. Where the disease is viral, only massive amounts of vitamin C will work — it alone kills viruses. Antibiotics are usually only given to control subsequent infections.*

Blood analysis is divided into three categories: biochemistry, microbiology and haematology.

Biochemistry readouts can be used to ascertain the mineral status of the blood. However for the purpose of blood analysis in performance horses the usual test involves electrolytes, enzymes and proteins. I would suggest that horse owners insist on having the biochemistry readout done occasionally just to see that the minerals and vitamins are in order.

Microbiology is used for the detection of organisms in the blood. If the horse is suffering from an infection and if antibiotics are to be used, a blood test will establish the sensitivity or resistance to such drugs. The advantage of using vitamin C therapeutically is that infections cannot be resistant to it.

Haematology is the complete red cell, white cell and platelet read out, detailed as follows:

Haemoglobin — HB
Red cell count — RCC
Packed cell volume — PCV (red cell to plasma ratio)
Mean corpuscular volume — MCV
Mean corpuscular haemoglobin concentration
— MCHC
Total white cells (leucocytes) — WCC

There are also neutrophils, basophils, eosonophils, lymphocytes, monocytes and platelets.

This explanation should enable the reader of a blood test to gain some idea of what the various initials mean. Further enlightenment can then be sought from the vet in charge.

One point should be borne in mind: laboratories can make mistakes. If a serious problem is diagnosed from a blood test, it would be wise to have a second sample taken and sent to an independent laboratory. In human medicine, quite different results have been obtained by different laboratories, and in the animal world more than one horse has been virtually condemned on a readout from one laboratory. Harry Shannon is particularly emphatic about this.

Many people have asked me, both here and in the United Kingdom, how we managed to get so many winners without blood tests half a century ago (we headed the trainers' list for a number of years). We rode out the horses that we looked after and could ride up to five in a day. One very soon learned by the feel of a horse whether it was fit or not.

When a horse first comes into work, possibly off grass, it is sluggish and apt to be uncoordinated. It is green, in other

words. Quite often it then goes through a stage of being just
plain silly. This is when they bang themselves about if not
ridden very steadily in their work. The final stage is when
they become really fit. Then much of its work occurs on hilly
roads and country, and the horse swings along with minimum
effort. *Then* we knew they were fit. This could take about two
and half months possibly, or more if the horse comes in too
gross and the condition has to be worked off it. This sequence
actually applies to almost any discipline and a great deal of
hard work goes into all the stages. I am indebted to Harry
Shannon and his booklet *Blood Analysis of Performance Horses*
for much of the information in this chapter. He was particularly adamant about having two tests done at different
laboratories, as suggested above.

Conclusion

The importance of vitamins and minerals and healthy food for any horse cannot be over-stated. All too often these days, especially at the time of writing — with the obsession about equine flu — good nutrition seems to be out of fashion and forgotten.

Throughout my life, and in this book, I have tried my hardest to get this point across. I believe that all horse owners should have their land analysed for its main mineral content, so they know what to do to give their horse the best diet possible. If they then buy or grow good, pure and unadulterated feed, good health will be the result.

Unfortunately, with many these days, this approach is all too rare — even at the lofty heights of the thoroughbred industry.

In the late 1990s, I gave a talk to about a hundred trainers and owners at Sydney's Randwick Racecourse — including some very prominent people indeed. I opened the proceedings by asking how many of them relied on pelleted feed to their horses. One of those attending — a fairly well-known group-one trainer — was among the eighty per cent of the audience who put their hand up. I asked him what was actually in this processed food he was giving to his charges. All he could say was that the contents were on the label (which did produce a slight laugh around the room). But at least he was honest.

Basically, if we rely heavily on processed food, we have no real idea of what our horses are getting. But we can be sure that they are often not getting the fresh and healthy food that they need to realise anywhere near their full potential. Horses we look after deserve food grown well on healthy land.

Healthy horses living on a healthy diet will be resistant to illness — or will be able to deal with it quickly if they do become ill. Relying on vaccination or medication is simply not the answer.

The reaction in late 2007 to equine flu was out of touch with reality. True, it is a great pity that the illness came into the country — but it is not an epidemic that brings death and destruction to the land. It is simply not a very serious illness. Horses are slightly unwell for a period (and so should be cared for and given a proper balanced diet while they recover — which they almost always do). This care is what all people who look after horses should be providing — their animals are a little sick, not caught up in a death-dealing epidemic!

Pat Coleby
Maldon, Victoria

Appendix

Firms supplying vitamins, minerals and other services or products

Pat Coleby
Consultant
91 Church Street
Maldon, Victoria 3463
Phone (03) 5475 2680

Soil analysis

Ted Mikail
SWEP Analytical Laboratories
PO Box 59D
Noble Park, Victoria 3174

Phone	(03) 9701 6007
Fax	(03) 9701 5712
Website	http://www.swep.com.au/

SWEP now have facilities to process soil samples from off-shore; enquire for details. SWEP include cobalt, sulphur, hydrogen and boron, and can include total phosphorus and aluminium. Costs are:

$110

$121 with total phosphorus

$132 with total alumunium

(*All* prices are GST inclusive and subject to change) This is a very competitive price for the extended service offered; those interested in cropping would be wise to have these extra items.

SWEP provides an easy to understand analysis, and are most helpful in discussing results. They now show the desired quantities of each item, which greatly assists the farmer's understanding of the results. The money (as above) should be sent with the sample. It takes about nine working days — this is quicker than most — for the result to be returned.

When sending up the analysis to SWEP (Ted Mikhail) ask him to send a copy of the results of the analysis to me (he has the address). When the result comes back to you, allow a day for my peculiar mail system and ring me on the above number and I will help with any measures that you may need to take, either on the farm or with your stock.

A soil sample is taken from the top 7 or 8 cm (about 4") of soil, from about thirty or more locations on the farm (whatever size) or one paddock. Take core samples with a stainless steel, poly pipe or something nonferous; *do not* use galvanised pipe, copper, worn out dairy pipes or any other metal — there have been some very strange results from doing this. Mix the samples thoroughly, remove any growing matter and fill a bag with about half a kilogram of the mixture, and send it for analysis. A stainless steel apple corer makes a very good substitute for the proper tool; it is exactly the right length and easy to manage!

On a large farm where there are several soil types it may be of benefit to take more than one sample, but this is not often necessary. Any number of samples may be sent, but each one must be paid for as above.

SWEP also do water analysis; the charge is $80. 500 ml of water should be sent in a *clean* unbreakable package. Ted Mikail recommends taking several samples from the well, bore or whatever over a day, mixing them thoroughly and sending 500 ml out of it.

Vitamins, minerals and horse gear

Equine Supplies
PO Box 182
Pendle Hill, New South Wales 2145
Phone   (02) 9688 3220
Fax   (02) 9636 9146
Ask for the catalogue; their prices are good and they stock a wide range. They sell yellow dusting sulphur, copper sulphate, cobalt sulphate and zinc sulphate, as do good fodder merchants.

APPLE CIDER VINEGAR

Nowadays nearly all fodder merchants carry unpasteurised organic cider vinegar, they have it in bulk and can fill small containers as well. The vinegar is usually triple or quadruple strength and can be diluted accordingly.

COD-LIVER OIL (Vitamin A and D)

This can be obtained from any fodder store. Vitamins, especially vitamin A, are destroyed by light. Buy in a dark container.

Equine supplies

Equinade, Hampton (Victoria)
Sceneys
17 Third Avenue
Sunshine, Victoria 3020

DOLOMITE

New South Wales
Mines at Mudgee

Tasmania
Circular Head

South Australia
Mines in Mt Gambier area

Victoria
Coopers, Bacchus Marsh (stockpiles Tantanalla dolomite)

Queensland
Flinders dolomite
Jock Banks
MS 509
West Plain Creek
Sarina, Queensland 4737
Phone (07) 4943 1386

Western Australia
K and P M Green
Newdegate

P G and M Paini & Sons
Kogonup
Fertiliser agents or fodder supplies deal with one mine or another.

COPRA MEAL

Organic Products Pty Ltd
PO Box 764
Kenmore, Queensland 4069
Phone (07) 3202 8722
Fax   (07) 3202 7754

GYPSUM

New South Wales
Moulamein
Jim McKee
PO Box 105
Wagga Wagga South, New South Wales 2650
Phone (02) 6926 2200

South Australia
Cooks Plains (near Tailem Bend)

Victoria
Horsham/Kerang area
Ask your agent.

SEAWEED PRODUCTS

Nutrimol
Phone (03) 9720 2266
Fax   (03) 9729 2288
They supply Vitagran seaweed meal.
Natrakelp
PO Box 1000
Maroochydore, Queensland 4558

Supplies seaweed meal (BFA certified).
VITEC seaweed meal and liquid is available from distributors.
Freecall   1800 622 345
Hugo and Helen Dissler
PO Box 26
The Patch, Victoria 3792
General suppliers
Phone 1800 622 345

EMU OIL

Mail order suppliers
Kyirong Emus
RMB 422, Strathlea
Creswick, Victoria 3363
Phone (03) 5476 6254
All lines.

BOX ONE

Made by:
Bestcare Foods Ltd
31 Fennel Street
North Parramatta, New South Wales 2150
Phone (02) 9820 7668

AERATION

John Dowling
Daylesford, Victoria 3460
Phone (04) 2835 3657
New Zealand Wanen's Equine Ltd
RD5 Christchurch
New Zealand
Phone (64) 3347 807

Minerals and vitamins to buy

Equine Supplies, see details previously.
Toll free   1800 463 952
Fax   (02) 9636 9146
All prices include GST.

VAM (vitamins, amino acids and minerals in liquid form)

Injections   100 ml bottle $25.15
Paste   30 g $14.40
This is good for all animals as an injection or for oral use.
VAM is a long-term pick up, and takes twenty-four hours to
start working. Always use with vitamin B12. It can be used,
say, as a boost for ewes coming up to lambing. They need
only 2 ml at a time, calves about 5 ml and full-grown cattle
10 ml, horses the same.

VITAMIN B1

100 ml bottle $11.83
Invaluable for photosensitised animals; check my books for
amounts.

VITAMIN B12

100 ml bottle $10.91
Use this with VAM, see above, or on its own. A sick calf can
have 5 ml of VAM and 5 ml of B12 in the same syringe. In
healthy animals, B12 on its own is often enough. Give 2 ml
for a sheep or lamb and 10 ml for a cow.

VITAMIN C (sodium ascorbate)

100 ml bottle $10.91
Get two or three bottles. Keeps for a long time in the fridge.
It works for snake and poison bites — a snakebitten cow

needs 50 ml each side of the neck; see my books for amounts. It should also be used for all illnesses where an antibiotic is given.

VITAMIN B15 (DADA)

Get this with the help of your vet. It is *very* useful to have on hand, particularly for liver problems. Read about it in my books. The price is available on application.

ASCORBIC ACID

Bulk vitamin C powder 2 kg $52.46

SODIUM ASCORBATE, non acidic vitamin C

2 kg $80.69 (bucket)

SYRINGES

Enquire for syringe prices.
Get some 30 ml syringes.
Get 1/2 or 3/4" needles, size 18 swg.
50 ml syringes make very good drenching guns. Always have several on hand.
Enquire about freight. Parts of New South Wales are freight free.

All the above vitamins are water-based and can, if used straight away, be put in the same syringe. There is no danger of overdose as there would be with oil-based vitamins such as, say, vitamin A, D and E. Stick to an exact dosage for them. Syringes and needles can be used again until they get blunt. Wash them out thoroughly first in cold water and then two or three times in boiling water. *Always swab with methylated spirits or similar.*

Check the supplier's catalogue for further items.

DROUGHT FEEDING

Many horse and other stock keepers do not realise that for any animal to live, it has to have solid food in its system. It is no good just getting expensive feeds that have been hammer milled or processed in some way. Failing all else, clean straw can be added to hay.

Even in a drought situation, many of us would be able to find edibles of many kinds in our gardens (as many goat owners could tell you!)

Remember, once a horse loses too much of its body condition, you will have a very hard and expensive time to restore it to something like its proper weight. During this time, quiet exercise can be carried on.

Acknowledgements

Thanks must go to:

Rhonda and John Baker, for their press cutting on horse deaths.

Dr Ray Biffen of the Australian Feed Company, Willoughby, New South Wales, for information on cotton-seed meal.

Annette Boyd, Swanpool who made me explain things better! Castlemaine Veterinary Clinic, and Alan Clark in particular, for sharing research and knowledge with me.

Caroline Coleby, my eldest daughter for checking the manuscript and clearing up anomalies, as well as giving general help and advice whenever I needed it.

Margaret Deeble, for printouts of SCIDS.

Hugh Coleby, my son, for help and suggestions with various parts of the text, and chapter ten in particular.

Shona Gilbert, for persisting with her Ross River fever

cases and bringing up the answers.

Ann Litzner for information on paniculitis.

Ted Mikhail, of SWEP Analytical Laboratories for clarifying innumerable soil problems.

Ray Mokaraka for persisting with the filly mentioned in the arnica section and saving her against all odds. We all learnt in that case.

Judy Mulholland, for suggestions.

Bianca Willoughby for some clarifications and suggestions — always much needed!

Also, thanks to the many others who have over the years sent in interesting material and had the courage to stick in there when their horses were condemned and bring them to life again, and above all, to the many horses I have worked with and enjoyed.

Bibliography

Adams, Ruth, *Complete Guide to All the Vitamins*, Larchmont Books, New York, 1971.

Agricultural Bulletin, USA, 1994.

Albrecht, W A, *The Albrecht Papers*, Acres, Austin, 1975.

American Farriers Journal, Brookfield, 1992.

Auerbach, Charlotte, *Science of Genetics*, Hutchinson Press, London, 1969.

Bairacli Levy, Juliette de, *Herbal Handbook for Farm and Stable*, Faber and Faber, London, 1952.

Balfour, E B, *The Living Soil and the Haughley Experiment*, Universe Books, New York, 1976.

Begley, Sharon, 'The End of Antibiotics', in *Newsweek*, 1994.

Bennett, Peter, 'No time like too late', lecture, 1967.

Biological Institute of Sydney, *Veterinary Treatment for Sick Animals*, 1930.

Bowling, Michael, 'The Paradigm has Shifted', *Arabian Horse News*, September/October 1997. Reprinted with permission of *Arabian Visions Magazine*, USA.

Brownlow, C V, *Gould's Medical Dictionary — Editors*, The Blakiston Company, Philidelphia, 1943.

Buist, Robert, *Orotates, Mineral Salts of Vitamin B13*, University of New South Wales, Sydney, 1978.

Burdon, Kenneth L, *Burdon's Microbiology*, Collier-Macmillan, New York, 1967.

Cetinkaya, B, Erdogan, H M, and Morgan, K L, 'Relationships between the presence of Johne's disease and farm and management factors in dairy cattle in England', in *Preventative Veterinary Medicine*, Volume 32, University of Liverpool, Liverpool, 1997.

Coleby, Pat, *Healthy Cattle Naturally*, Landlinks Press, Collingwood, 2002.

Colloidal Silver, *A Literature Review: Coloidal Silver Uses*, Clear Lakes Press, Washington, 26 February 1998.

CSIRO (Commonwealth Scientific and Industry Research Organisation), *Rural Research Bulletins*, various.

Davis, Adelle, *Let's Get Well*, Allen and Unwin, London, 1972.

Dettman, Glenn; Kalokerinos, A; and Dettman, I; *Vitamin C, Nature's Miraculous Healing Missile*, Veritas Press, Melbourne, 1993.

Dilling, Walter J, *Clinical Pharmacology*, Cassell, London, 1960.

Dowling, Ralph M, and Mackenzie, I, *Poisonous Plants: A Field Guide*, Department of Primary Industries Information Series, Brisbane, 1993.

Everist, Selwyn P, *Poisonous Plants in Australia*, Angus and Robertson, Sydney, 1981.

Fitzherbert, John, 'Zinc Supplements' interview with Norman Swan, 2 April 2001.

Fitzwygram, F (Bart), *Horses and Stables*, Longman, Green and Company, London, 1880.

Fukuoka, Masanobu, *The One Straw Revolution*, Rodale Press, Emmaus, 1978.

Fukuoka, Masanobu, *The Road Back to Nature: Regaining Paradise Lost*, Acres USA, Kansas City, 1989.

Glass, Justine, *Earth Heals Everything: The Story of Biochemistry*, Peter Owen, London, 1958.

Goodman, Louis S. and Gillman, Alfred, *The Pharmacological Basis of Therapeutics*, Macmillan, New York, 1970.

Gregg, Charles T, *The Plague: An Ancient Disease in the Twentieth Century*, University of New Mexico, Abuquerque, 1986.

Grieve, M, *Modern Herbal I and II*, Penguin Books, Harmondsworth, 1971.

Hahnemann, Samuel, *Organon of the Rational Art of Healing*, Dresden, 1810.

Hayes, Horace, *Veterinary Notes for Horse Owners*, Hurst and Blackett Ltd, London, 1906.

Howard, Albert, *Agricultural Testament*, Oxford University Press, New York and London, 1943.

Hubberd, C E, *Grasses*, Penguin Books, Harmondsworth, 1972.

Hungerford, T, *Diseases of Livestock*, McGraw-Hill, Sydney, 1951.

Jarvis, D C, *Folk Medicine*, White Lion Publishers, London, 1958 (various handbooks on this subject, all with similar names).

Jensen, Bernard and Anderson, Mark, *Empty Harvest*, Avery, New York, 1973.

Johnson, Philip J, and Mrad, Dawn, 'Equine Protozoal

Myeloencephalitis', *Equine Internal Medicine*, University of Missouri, Columbia, 9 December 1995.

Kalokerinos, Archie, *Every Second Child*, Thomas Nelson, Melbourne, 1974.

Kalokerinos, Archie, and Dettman, G, 'Vitamin C and Cancer', paper presented at the International Association of Cancer Victims and Friends, Melbourne, 1979.

Kessler, J, 'Elements Mineraux Chez le Chevre, Donne de Base et Apports Recommands', Paper presented at ITOVIC INRA International Symposium on Feeding Systems for Goats, Tours, 1981.

Kinsey, Neal, and Walters, Charles, *Hands-On Agronomy*, Acres USA, Kansas City, 1993.

Lamand, M, 'Metabolisme et Besoins en Oligo-elements des Chevres', Paper presented at ITOVIC INRA, International Symposium on Feeding Systems for Goats, Tours, 1981.

Leahy, J, *Use and Abuse of Drugs*, University of Western Australia.

McCabe, Ed, *O₂xygen Therapies: A New Way to Approach Disease*, Energy Publications, New York, 1988.

Mackenzie, Ross A, *Studies on Calcium Deficiencies in Horses, Induced by Grazing Tropical Grasses Containing Oxalates*, Queensland Department of Primary Industry, Australia, 1984.

MacLeod, George, *A Veterinary Materia Medica and Clinical Repertory*, C W Daniel and Company Ltd, Saffron Waldon, 1995.

Marston, Hedley R, and Robertson, Brailsford, 'Utilisation of Sulphur by Animals', *CSIR Bulletin*, No 39, Australia, 1928.

Martindale, William, *The Extra Pharmacopoea*, Pharmaceutical Press, London, 1982.

Moore, James, *Outlines of Veterinary Homeopathy*, Henry

Turner and Co., Manchester and London, 1874.

Moskowveitch, Richard, MD, 'Immunisations: A Dissenting View', Lecture 8 in *Dissent in Medicine, Nine Doctors Speak Out*, Contemporary Books Inc, Chicago, 1984.

Passwaters, Richard A, *Selenium as Food and Medicine: What You Need to Know*, Keats Publishing, New Canaan, 1980.

Podhajsky, Alois, *My Horses, My Teachers*, J A Allen, London, 1997.

References include extracts from *British Medical Journal* 280/1335. *Australia Veterinary Journals* 47, 48, 66, 443 and 52/199 and *Victorian Veterinary Proceedings*, page 144.

Russel, Mark; Scott, D; and Hope, W; *Moldy Corn Poisoning in Horses*, Purdue University, reported in *Acres USA*, February 1995.

Schuessler, Dr W H, *Biochemic Handbook*, New Era Laboratories, London, 1997.

Shannon, H D, *Blood Analysis of Performance Horses*, Max A Harrell, 1994.

Shepparton Veterinary Clinic Newsletter, 'Information on Anti-inflammatories', April 1997.

Silver education coalition, *Colloidal Silver Handbook*, Salt Lake City, 1971.

Smith, J D; Jordan, R M; and Nelson, M L; 'Tolerance of Ponies to High Levels of Dietary Copper' in *Journal of Animal Science*, Vol 41, No 6, University of Minnesota, St Paul, 1975.

Spier, Dr Sharon, *HYPP — Another Look*, taken from a 1989 research project by the University of California and updated from research by Dr Stone in 1991 at the same University. Published in the *American Quarter Horse Journal*.

Stone, Irwin T, *The Healing Factor: Vitamin C Against Disease*, Grosset and Dunlap, New York, 1974.

Technical Data Sheet: Report on H_2O_2 and Colloidal Silver in *Sanitation of Stock Drinking Water*, Integrity Products (Australasia) Pty Ltd.

Turner, Newman, *Fertility Farming*, Faber and Faber, London, 1950.

Viral Diseases of Horses, Coital Exanthema, veterinary print-out, no attribution, Institute of Agriculture, University of Minnesota.

Voisin, Andre, *Grass Productivity*, Island Press, Washington DC, 1959.

Voisin, Andre, *Soil, Grass and Cancer*, Acres USA, Kansas City, 1999.

Volker, L and Steinberg, W, *The Vitamin Requirements of Goats*.

Itovic INRA — Symposium International.

Wallach, Dr Joel, *Dead Doctors Don't Lie*, tape.

Willis, Harold, 'Roots', in *Acres USA*, December 1994.

Yiamouyiannis, John, *Fluoride, The Ageing Factor*, Health Action Press, Delaware, 1993.

Index

C

D

T

U

V

W

ALSO FROM HACHETTE AUSTRALIA

WILD HORSE DIARIES

Lizzie Spender

From a helicopter skimming above the trees in the immense outback of Western Australia, Lizzie Spender looked out and saw wild horses galloping below. She fell in love with a chestnut colt with a crooked white blaze. She was told she could take it home, if she could find it, catch it and train it — a virtually impossible quest.

This offer would fulfil her dream of a lifetime, but there were other obstacles at every turn. And as Lizzie discovered, finding the horse again was only the start of the story.

'Extraordinary'
Sunday Telegraph

'sharp insights'
Sydney Morning Herald

'A truly inspiring adventure'
Daily Mail

'Lizzie's story about the wild brumbies in Australia is a
wonderful example of how the horse can give us so much
— and how they can virtually change our lives.'

Monty Roberts

LIZZIE SPENDER

WILD HORSE
DIARIES

A true outback adventure story about
realising the dream of a lifetime